IMAGES
of England

CANTERBURY
1945-1975

The Regal Cinema in St George's Place during 1949. The side wall was of recent construction, following a direct hit in October 1942, when the adjoining Regal Ballroom was destroyed. The only consequence for the surviving and repaired cinema portion of the complex was the loss of its once symmetrical frontage.

IMAGES
of England

CANTERBURY
1945-1975

Compiled by
Paul Crampton

TEMPUS

First published 2002
Copyright © Paul Crampton, 2002

Tempus Publishing Limited
The Mill, Brimscombe Port,
Stroud, Gloucestershire, GL5 2QG

ISBN 0 7524 2457 2

Typesetting and origination by
Tempus Publishing Limited
Printed in Great Britain by
Midway Colour Print, Wiltshire

Caption for the front cover: *The residents of Rosemary Lane pose for the camera, during their Coronation celebrations in the first week of June 1953. Many other streets across Canterbury held similar events, organizing their own street parties, parades, pageants and crowning ceremonies (see chapter three).*

A parked delivery van on the Kings Bridge causes problems for other road users, *c.* 1950. This bottleneck had been troublesome since the 1930s, even though traffic levels were much lower then. The surrounding buildings appear very much as they do today.

Contents

A typical cathedral view, taken from the blitzed St George's Street during the 'buddleia years' of the late 1940s. The bombing had opened up unobstructed views of the cathedral from this largely flattened quadrant of the city, where buddleia, willow herb and tree saplings all grew unchecked.

Acknowledgements

The vast majority of the photographic material reproduced herein comes from two main archives: that of the Fisk-Moore Studio and Messenger Group Newspapers. I am grateful to the latter for their continued support and permission to use their material.

I would also like to acknowledge the help of the following for supplying photographs: Patrick Brown, Canterbury Archaeological Trust; the late Dr William Urry; the Reverend David L. Cawley; the late David Cousins; Ben May, Invicta Motors; Mr W.E. Haynes, Dick Brown, and Canterbury Museums.

The introduction and much of the material in the first half of this volume was originally intended for inclusion in the unpublished Meresborough Books title, *Canterbury in the Early 1950s*. This was to be the last in a trilogy of books concerning the re-planning of our city in the aftermath of the bombing, begun in the title *Canterbury after the Blitz* and continued in *Canterbury in the late 1940s – The 'Buddleia Years'*. I am pleased to be finally able to complete the story.

Introduction

In March 1951, Canterbury City Council approved a twenty-year development plan for the rebuilding of the blitzed city and the provision of a new road system. This had been prepared by the City Architect, Mr L. Hugh Wilson, under the terms of the 1947 Town and Country Planning Act. There was considerable opposition to the plan, mainly from the Citizens Association (formerly known as the Canterbury Citizens Defence Association), who opposed the amount of 34 acres of compulsory purchase to be included in it. The Corporation had stated quite clearly that this land acquisition was essential to the plan's implementation, whereas the Citizens Association preferred to see redevelopment along the lines of private enterprise.

Throughout December 1951 and January 1952, the *Kentish Gazette* published a series of articles prepared by Hugh Wilson, to explain to the public in detail the main elements of the Development Plan. One of the concerns of those opposed to the plan was that its implementation would destroy the 'medieval character' of the city. In direct response to this, Mr Wilson gave his interpretation of 'medieval character'. He stated that it was more to do with 'the shape and form of the spaces created by a plan, the relationship between the spaces and the buildings around them', rather than 'the superficial appearance of the individual buildings' (quaint gables, old tiled roofs, half timbering to walls and leaded windows).

These remarks upset a lot of people, judging by the amount and content of letters published in the *Kentish Gazette* during the following weeks. One correspondent condemned Mr Wilson for his 'pretentious, pseudo-technical tarradiddle'. The *Gazette* itself was well known for its opposition to the Wilson Plan, as well as its predecessor, the eccentric and rejected Holden Plan. In fairness to Hugh Wilson and the City Council, the paper withheld any editorial comment until the aforementioned series of articles had been completed. However, once the last one had been published, the *Gazette* printed several uncompromisingly critical editorials that openly lobbied for the plan's rejection. They were particularly unforgiving with regard to Canterbury City Council, especially those members, (the vast majority,) who had once vehemently opposed compulsory purchase, but now wholeheartedly embraced the Wilson Plan. To press the point home, they quoted the words of two current council members who had changed their tune and now achieved high office. In September 1947, Councillor Barrett opposed a recommendation that the central area of the city be acquired by exercising powers of compulsory purchase. He said, 'Let us go slow; put back or reject these proposals, knowing full well that things are changing very rapidly today. In the near future, we shall be asked how far can we cut down our plans and develop on the lines of private enterprise'. By early 1952, Councillor Barrett was Sheriff of Canterbury, Chairman of the City Council Town Planning Committee and a strong supporter of the Wilson Plan. Moreover, in September 1946, Councillor Jennings had spoken passionately against the concept of wholesale compulsory purchase. Now he was the Mayor of Canterbury and another staunch supporter of the Wilson Plan. In fact, of his former anti-compulsory purchase colleagues and their continued fight, he remarked, 'The fact that the Citizens Association discussed the scheme without being aware of all the facts is just too bad. We [the council] have a very good case'.

The Citizens Association had indeed continued to oppose the compulsory purchase element of the Wilson Plan. Some 232 objections had been sent to Harold Macmillan, Minister of Housing and Local Government. Consequently, a public enquiry was held over five days during February 1952, to hear those objections. The enquiry was conducted by Mr S. Knight, one of the ministry's inspectors, and the case for the Corporation was conducted by the Town Clerk, Mr John Boyle. On the first day, Mr Boyle made some 'sensational allegations', the *Gazette* reported. He stated that of the 232 so-called registered objections, some had been duplicated, some were submitted by Messrs Amos and Dawton without authorization, and two letters written by the same firm were 'false documents' within the meaning of the Forgery Act! This set the tone for what proved to be a lively enquiry, with the brunt of the attack being borne by Mr Wilson. Ultimately, the minister came down on the side of the Corporation and the Wilson Plan. The City Council was vindicated. However the plan had already been put into operation and construction work begun in St George's Street some months before. By the end of 1952, new buildings could be found on both sides of the street.

With regards to the old buildings of Canterbury, the fear of significant demolition was another concern of the Citizens Association, and in particular their chairman, Anthony Swaine. Hugh Wilson attempted to reassure the conservationists in his first *Kentish Gazette* article that no scheduled ancient monuments or Grade II listed buildings would be affected by the implementation of the development plan. John Boyle reiterated this point on the first day of the public enquiry. This was true, as far as the situation in 1951 was concerned, when there were only 163 Grade II listed buildings in the whole of Canterbury. However this did not mean that no important or cherished structures were threatened by the implementation of the Wilson Plan. As far as the Central Development Area was concerned, that is the 34-acre area to be purchased compulsorily, conservationists had real reason for concern. In late 1951, the entire length of the Whitefriars north wall and part of the west wall had been demolished. Although extensively patched up in the eighteenth and nineteenth centuries, these walls still contained in-situ medieval fabric. This included blocked windows, and a doorway that may have once been the west door of the long-lost Whitefriars Church. The main body of St George's Church was demolished in stages during 1951 and 1952. There is no doubt that medieval fabric was destroyed here. Also bulldozed in 1952 were the old burial ground, and the adjacent St George's Primary School in Canterbury Lane. Another 1952 victim was a row of four late eighteenth and nineteenth-century cottages in Burgate Lane, which were built from Caen stone blocks. Beforehand, Dorothy Gardiner had protested against their loss on the grounds that they were a rebuild of an Elizabethan stone house which had stood on the same site. Moreover, she claimed that original Elizabethan work still existed in the structure. However at the public enquiry, Mr Boyle stated that the rebuilt cottages were unfit for habitation, and would be pulled down as they posed a danger to the public! Yet-another early 1950s victim was a large and handsome Georgian house at No.1 Watling Street, which stood just inside the city wall near to the Riding Gate.

Thus, the 1950s got underway with new buildings appearing, old buildings disappearing and disputes between the corporation and conservationists or property owners. This set a pattern that would be repeated many times over the next twenty-five years. Canterbury in the mid-1950s saw the rebuilding continue, but slowed by a financial crisis so serious that the whole concept of compulsory purchase for the Central Development Area had to be re-thought. Councillor Barrett's words from 1946 were indeed prophetic.

One
The Late 1940s

The north end of the narrow Mercery Lane as it opens out into The Buttermarket, with the cathedral's Christchurch Gate beyond, c. 1948. In the foreground on the left is part of the complex for Lefevre & Hunt and on the right, the tobacconist and confectioner E.A. Hart at No. 15 Mercery Lane. Only six years before, the incendiary fires of the June 1942 Baedeker Raid were halted barely fifty yards to the right of this scene. With the wealth of timber-framed buildings here, imagine how much worse the Blitz could have been.

Archaeologist Dr Sheppard Frere cleans up one of a series of medieval hearths discovered beneath a blitzed site on the south side of Burgate Street. The years between the bombing of 1942 and the rebuilding of the early 1950s offered a unique opportunity to discover much about Canterbury's past, in particular the then little-known Roman period. However at this time, all archaeological investigations took place in the summer only and were undertaken by gifted amateurs, under the guidance of the Canterbury Excavation Committee.

An excavated cellar in St George's Street, once beneath the stationers W.H. Smith & Son. Archaeologists were amazed to discover that the cellar's east wall (centre) was a re-used Roman wall, once part of a larger public bath complex. The curved brick wall of the post-medieval cellar stairwell is on the far left. When the cellar was first created, the excavators must have encountered this substantial wall and incorporated it, rather than go through all the effort of digging it out.

The war-damaged premises of blind makers, H. Amey & Sons, just off Ivy Lane, c. 1946. The picture, taken from Lower Chantry Lane, would not have been possible prior to the demolition of the blitzed Payne-Smith Schools. The Amey's premises, once an oast house, had lost its roof in the raid of 1 June 1942, but continued to operate from the undamaged floors, where huge sewing machines turned acres of material into window blinds. A new roof was added in the same year (see page 126).

A Blitz-damaged shop and its undamaged neighbour in Lower Bridge Street, during 1949. The former was once hairdressers Herbert Santer (No. 14), the latter, New Florists that was run by Mr P.E. Jackson at No. 14a (see page 32). The damaged building had only escaped the ruthless post-blitz demolition purge because the shops either side were intact. Nevertheless, it would be pulled down in the early 1950s. The florists hung on until 1969, when its demolition was required for the second stage of the city's ring road (see page 116).

Field Marshal Earl Montgomery takes the salute at the British Legion parade, in 1948. Standing next to him is the current Mayor, Alderman Mrs Hews. Behind is the British Legion House at No. 7 New Dover Road, with the premises of Abbott Bros. Dairies (No. 15) just visible beyond. The British Legion building would be demolished in the late 1950s to make way for the new offices and showrooms for Caffyns (see page 92). The Abbott Bros. premises survive today.

A gathering from St Augustine's College holding a religious ceremony in the ruined crypt of St Augustine's Abbey, as part of their centenary celebrations in 1948. The college was run from buildings surviving from the medieval abbey complex, supplemented by Victorian additions, in a medieval style. Soaring up behind the abbey ruins is the Canterbury Technical College & County Technical School for Boys. This late eighteenth-century building had been the original Kent & Canterbury Hospital until 1937 (see page 123).

Number 1 Lady Wootton's Green: an imposing Georgian house, almost swallowed up by the adhering vegetation. In the late 1940s, it was the dwelling of Miss Wiltshier, Miss Kemp and Mr Jack Usher. At the time, this was the only house left standing in Lady Wootton's Green. Others, damaged in the June 1942 Blitz, were pulled down despite there being ample scope for repair and renovation. The surviving house had been built onto the ruins of the medieval St Augustine's Almonry Chapel, although the surviving medieval fabric was largely hidden by Georgian plaster.

A procession from St Augustine's College passing along Broad Street during 1948, as part of their centenary celebrations. Their destination is the cathedral for a service of thanksgiving. The tail end of the procession is just coming out of Lady Wootton's Green, where the sole blitz-surviving house, mentioned above, can be seen. Centre right are three remaining houses in Broad Street, which can still be found today. Others on either side were demolished in the thorough post-blitz clear up, despite having suffered only minor damage.

The empty St Mary Bredin School in Rhodaus Town, closed in 1940 and photographed nearly ten years later. It was built in 1860 on top of a small piece of raised ground, thought to be the remains of a Roman burial mound. During the war years, the former school had become one of Canterbury's British Restaurants, providing reasonably priced three-course lunches. Now it was vacant and looking for another use. By 1953, the building and surrounding land had been bought up by Rootes Ltd, who owned the adjacent garage complex. Today, it is the used car centre for Canterbury Motor Company.

Another empty building, the former British Oak public house, on the corner of Rosemary Lane and Church Lane St Mildred's. The pub had closed as long ago as 1931, and stood empty and boarded up until finally being demolished in 1948. The timber-framed roof and jettied upper storey of this seventeenth-century building can be seen being dismantled. Even then, the brick-built ground-floor walls were retained well into the 1950s as a secure perimeter to the site, which eventually became a surface car park.

City firemen tackle a dramatic blaze at the premises of Invicta Motor Co., in Lower Bridge Street, c. July 1949. A petrol tanker had reversed into the garage area and the driver paused to light a cigarette before dismounting. The resulting explosion killed the unfortunate driver and spread blazing fuel throughout that part of the premises, and up into the roof. It was amazing that no Invicta staff were badly affected by the incident.

The fire chief examines the smouldering interior of the Invicta garage, shortly after the fire has been quenched. Left, the burnt out petrol tanker with its cab roof peeled off, as a result of the explosion. To the right is a pair of brand new Ford Anglia saloons, both damaged in the fire. Fortunately, damage to the building was comparatively light and within months, repairs had returned things to normal. In the early 1960s the Lower Bridge Street premises, then a collection of small garages and converted houses, would be replaced in stages by a new purpose-built complex (see page 90).

The burnt-out shell of St George's Church, standing within its well-overgrown churchyard, in the late 1940s. Chestnut paling fences surround the buddleia-filled cellars along what was once the busy shopping thoroughfare of St George's Street. No one could agree on the fate of the ruin. Its immediate post-blitz demolition had been halted by a concerned cathedral canon in June 1942. The 1945 Holden Development Plan also wanted it retained, as a war memorial. Its successor, the 1947 Wilson Plan, wanted it gone. In the end, a compromise saw the tower only retained and restored (see page 44).

A unique view of the inside of the St George's Church ruin, showing a number of lost medieval features. The south wall (centre and right) fronts St George's Street. The blocked door to the right once led into a projecting vestry, demolished in the mid-nineteenth century for street improvements. Centre view are two lovely sedilia, once used by the officiating priest and his deacon. Left is the east wall, against which the altar stood until 1872, when the church was expanded northwards. The south wall was demolished in 1951.

Two
Demolition in the 1950s

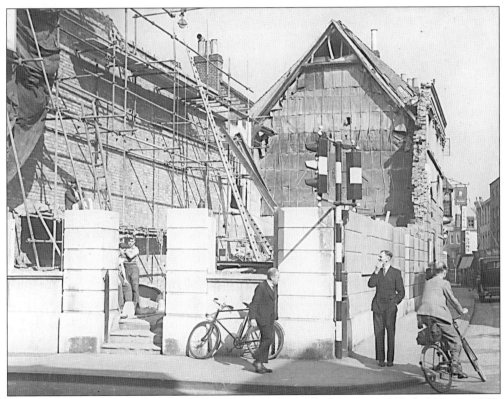

The partially demolished Guildhall, on the corner of Guildhall Street and High Street in 1950. What remained at this time were the stuccoed ground floor walls of the main hall, up to a height of ten feet. Moreover at the north end, the Mayor's Parlour still existed in its entirety. Nothing more was done until 1955, when these remains were finally removed and a shoe shop built on the site. The remains of a twelfth-century vaulted undercroft can still be viewed beneath the shop today.

An extensive property at No. 57 North Lane, being dismantled, c. 1951. It was one of only two buildings from a row of superb fifteenth to seventeenth-century properties to have survived the post-blitz demolition programme. The left hand section which fronted North Lane had been rebuilt in the early nineteenth century, to provide a more substantial third storey, thus giving the roof a shallower pitch. Today, it is the site of the narrow North Lane car park.

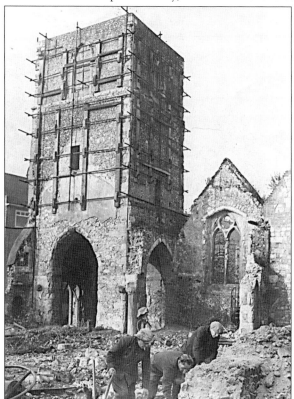

The sad sight of the blitzed shell of St George's Church finally being pulled down in October 1952. The demolition ended a ten-year battle between those who wanted to destroy the whole church, and those who would have liked it conserved. Once completed, the carved stonework that once made up the window jambs and tracery was carted up to Littlebourne Road, where a garden wall was made from them. Restoration of the remaining tower began in 1953.

An early 1950s pre-slum clearance view of a row of cottages at numbers 267 to 273 (odds only), Sturry Road. Left is the Rising Sun public house, which was to be retained. The houses were of simple timber framed construction, with weather-boarded façades, an uncommon sight in Canterbury. They were condemned as the wooden frame was found to be in a bad state of decay. Following demolition, a single bungalow was built on the site.

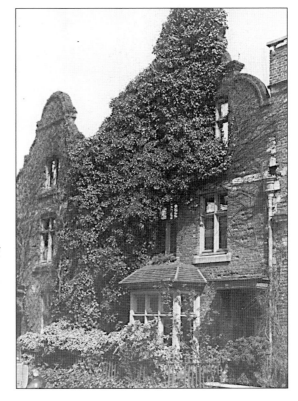

The ivy-clad shells of two Jacobean Dutch-gabled houses, at numbers 18 and 19 Watling Street, in 1953. The roofs and interiors had been lost in the Blitz of June 1942 and, considering how ruthless the post-blitz clearance operation had been, it is amazing that these remains were not touched. Nevertheless, their demolition came shortly after this picture was taken, although the site remained empty for another eighteen years! A neo-Georgian office block now stands on the plot (see page 125).

A pair of shops at numbers 47 and 48 St Peter's Street in 1953, just after a small fire in the roofs had been extinguished. Until 1952, Woolworth's had occupied both shops, but then relocated to brand new premises in St George's Street (see page 40). These shops were entirely timber-framed and probably of early nineteenth-century date. What appears to be a brick built frontage, is in fact mathematical tiles arranged to imitate bricks. The fire was used as an excuse to demolish both properties (and a third one, just seen to the right). New shop buildings replaced them.

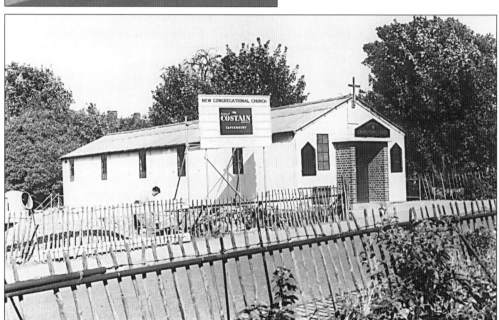

The temporary Congregational Church in Watling Street, during the spring of 1954, surrounded by overgrown bombsites. The original church had also been a victim of the 1942 Blitz. Work was now about to begin on a permanent replacement church, as the hoarding announces. The temporary church was then to be dismantled and sold to Tyler Hill for continued use as a village hall. Sadly, the 'permanent' 1950s church was pulled down in early 2001, to be replaced by the fourth version being built on the opposite side of the road.

A rear view of the 1928-built Machine Bakery, operated by Nicholas Kingsman Ltd, in Canterbury Lane. By 1953, the redevelopment of St George's Street and the lanes feeding it had reached an advanced stage. The few buildings surviving the Blitz in the area, including the bakery, would have to be demolished to make way for road widening and new shops. Its modernist, flat-roofed concrete construction was why it was able to come through the wartime firebombing, but it could not resist the tide of progress, represented by the new David Greig premises visible behind.

The Longmarket on 12 October 1956. Pre-fabricated shops erected here in 1947 mingle with the few blitz-surviving buildings on the site. One temporary structure – until recently occupied by the National Provincial Bank – is being dismantled, following the completion of the bank's superb new premises in St George's Street, just off camera to the right (see page 44). The remaining pre-fabs, together with the few pre-war buildings left, would be demolished in 1959 to make way for the new Longmarket shopping development (see page 89).

The last remaining girder from the now redundant Elham Valley Line railway bridge falls into the River Stour below in April 1955. The bridge, built to carry double track, had only supported a single railway line following the downgrading of the Elham Valley Line in the early 1930s. The line closed completely in 1947, and the track was lifted from the Canterbury end of the line during the following year. The iron bridge that once carried the line over the road at Wincheap had been taken down in March 1955.

The imposing Regency period Woodville House at the top end of Wincheap, being pulled down, c. 1957. Up until then, it had been known as the Woodville Homes for Children, with Miss G.M. Pearson as matron. Following demolition, Woodville Close was laid out on the site to serve a new development of flats (see page 110). Just visible to the right is the chimney of Thannington water pumping station. The last remains of that charming building were finally removed in 2001.

Canterbury Scouts stand to attention in front of the new Mayor's Parlour in Tower House, just off St Peter's Place, in October 1954. This is a selective enlargement of a more general view, so as to highlight the houses on the opposite side of the road. Built in the 1830s along with most of the other properties in St Peter's Place, these three houses would soon be compulsorily purchased by the City Council and pulled down. This was to free the site for a new road junction between the proposed ring road and cross-city relief road. Neither road scheme was ever completed.

Old houses being demolished on the east side of North Lane in February 1956, as part of a night-time civil defence exercise. They were coming down to allow North Lane to be widened at this location and to extend the car park, which had been created following the demolition of other older properties (see page 18). The buildings seen here on the west side of the lane remain today.

The late-Victorian porch to St Andrew's Church, squeezed in between existing buildings on the south side of The Parade, pictured in 1953. It allowed access to the red-brick Georgian church almost hidden behind. Long since redundant as a place of worship, St Andrew's was demolished in 1956, for an extension to the adjoining Westminster Bank.

The rear gateway to the Corn Exchange and Longmarket complex, during its partial demolition in early 1957. The Corn Exchange was badly damaged in June 1942 and the main structure demolished shortly afterwards. The undamaged rear gateway in Burgate was retained, largely because it contained public conveniences. The last traces of it were removed in 1959.

The forlorn sight of the last remains of the ancient Fleur de Lis Hotel in the High Street being removed in March 1958. The eighteenth-century façade being demolished here hid an ancient timber-framed structure, with elements dating back to the fourteenth century. The demise of 'The Fleur' was a serious defeat for Canterbury conservationists, who lobbied hard for its retention.

A rare picture from the mid-1950s, of a little remembered house that once stood in St George's Place, immediately adjacent to the Regal Cinema (see page 2). It was known as St George's House and dated from the late Georgian period. Its extensive grounds had been sold off in the early 1950s for a large garage and showroom building for Martin Walters Ltd (just visible left). It finished its life converted into offices and was finally pulled down in 1958 for a further extension to the same garage premises.

The northernmost section of Hookers Watermill being dismantled by hand, in July 1958. It stood on the junction of St Stephen's Road and The Causeway, and was being removed to make way for an improved road junction and pavement. The central timbered section of the mill – the remains of which are visible to the right – was destroyed by fire on the night of Tuesday 9 June 1954. The southernmost brick-built section also perished in the blaze. In more recent years, a facsimile of the lost watermill has been constructed on the site, as a development of retirement flats.

Blitz-surviving shops on the east side of Butchery Lane in July 1959, just prior to their demolition. They backed onto the Longmarket site and were being removed for the comprehensive redevelopment of the whole area. The single-storey shops either side of the 1930s Court and Cooke premises, both once had timber framed and jettied upper storeys that had survived the Blitz. Those above the Brighter Homes and Finnis Bakers premises (right) were removed in about 1950. The upper storeys to the shop on the left were destroyed by fire in January 1955 (see page 54).

A charming study from September 1959, of the lost oast house in Dover Street. Originally built in 1811, the oast re-used the side walls of an earlier structure, which had itself been constructed from re-used Caen stone blocks. It is likely that the stone was recovered from the nearby ruins of St Augustine's Abbey in the years following its dissolution in 1538 (see page 12). Sadly, the oast had gone by the end of the year to make way for a rear extension to Martin Walter's Garage complex fronting St George's Place.

A rear view of the terraced houses on the south side of New Ruttington Lane in 1958, photographed as part of a pre-slum clearance survey. These houses had been built in the 1810s and '20s for the families of the personnel serving at the nearby army barracks. Similar houses were also built in the adjacent, newly created streets of Military Road, Union Street, Artillery Street and Artillery Gardens, all of which are featured in later chapters. Those pictured here were demolished in late 1959 and replaced by a low-rise development of flats.

The beginning of slum clearance on the north side of Union Street, in January 1959. These houses were part of the same early-nineteenth century scheme as those in New Ruttington Lane (seen on the previous page). Demolition was being carried out in stages, followed by the redevelopment of that particular block, before moving on to the clearance of the next area. Following the demolition of its north side, Union Street was widened and became the main access route into Canterbury from the Sturry Road. Tobin's Garage was then built on the north side of the widened road (see page 91). The south side of Union Street was pulled down in 1962 (see page 72).

Yet more houses being pulled down to extend garage premises in late 1959. These, on the south side of Dover Street have been stripped prior to demolition for the new garage and filling station for Bligh Bros. Ltd (see page 91). The oast featured on page 27, situated on the opposite side of the road, was being demolished at the same time. The new Bligh Bros. garage would only survive until the early 1970s, giving way for an office block development that, ultimately, never materialised. Today, the site is part of the Holman's Meadow surface car park.

Three
Coronation
Celebrations

Residents of Rosemary Lane march behind an accordion player during the Coronation celebrations of early June 1953. The bunting, union flags and patriotic banners were to be found decorating most of Canterbury's residential streets at the time. The early nineteenth-century terraced houses of Rosemary Lane would be the subject of a slum clearance scheme in 1962. Only the Cardinal's Cap public house – just visible on the left – would escape the bulldozer. Part of Williamson's Tannery can be seen at the far end of the street, as it can be today.

Children in fancy dress pose for the camera on the green just off Davidson Road, June 1953. This road was part of a small estate of exactly one hundred identical pre-fabricated houses, laid out in 1946 and '47. Some of the pre-fabs can be seen behind the gathering. Most of the children came from this estate, which also included Temple Road, Bishops Way, Fisher Road and Lang Road. A young girl and boy posing as bride and groom seem delighted to be the centre of attention, although the bridesmaid, just to their right, does not seem to be so happy about the occasion.

The happy, smiling residents of Gordon Road and Martyr's Field Road march to the music of a barrel organ, during their Coronation celebrations. Only one small boy to the right seems to have noticed the cameraman. The picture was taken in Gordon Road, just south of the East Station and railway coal yard. Also visible on the other side of the main line, is the late-Victorian St Andrew's Presbyterian Church (see page 123). Sadly, both coal yard and church are only a memory today.

The residents of Artillery Street gather for posterity at the west end of their street. A number of the children are clutching plates, no doubt in anticipation of the treats to be provided later by their parents and neighbours. A little girl, dressed as the queen, proudly waves from the back of the group. The terraced houses on the right would perish in 1962, whilst those on the left of the street would last until 1968 before being demolished. The buildings in Northgate beyond, remain today.

On 2 June 1953, the residents of Querns Road celebrated the Coronation by crowning their own queen. Because it was raining that day, their 'Coronation' also took place in an abbey, St Augustine's. The oldest resident, the ninety-seven-year-old Anna Edwards (also known as Granny Edwards), places the crown on the head of their queen, fourteen-year-old Eileen Morris. Now Eileen Burfield, she still has the sash with 'Miss Coronation' on it. Sadly, Granny Edwards died later in the same year.

Patriotic bunting being put up in Northgate during May 1953. Before the widening of Union Street in 1960, this was part of the main route into Canterbury from Sturry Road. Two lost public houses are visible. On the left is the Two Brothers at No. 91 Northgate, which closed in the mid 1960s. Opposite is the Model Tavern at No. 54 that closed its doors as recently as the late 1980s. Just beyond the Model Tavern, are three properties (numbers 55 to 57), which would be demolished in the late 1950s, to provide a car park for the pub.

These proud people have just won second prize in the 1953 Canterbury carnival contest for the best decorated vehicle. An appropriately patriotic floral crown tops the Ford estate car. The gentleman is Mr P.E. Jackson, proprietor of New Florists, who traded from No. 14a Lower Bridge Street (see pages 11 and 116). Presumably, the very fashionably dressed lady is Mrs Jackson.

Part of the premises of Rootes Ltd – automobile engineers in Rhodaus Town – freshly painted and decorated in preparation for the Coronation. There was much friendly competition between commercial premises as to who could come up with the best decorations. Rootes made a special effort, as their premises overlooked the city moat and wall where the city's official pageant would soon take place (see page 35).

Ladies outfitters Baldwin & Son in the High Street shows off its impressive Coronation illuminations one evening in June 1953. As is the case with many buildings in the unblitzed part of the main street, Baldwin's was much older than it first appeared to be. Behind the 'modern' façade existed two medieval three-storey timber-framed structures. The unaltered rear elevations gave away the building's true age (see page 80). Despite its great age, Baldwin's was demolished in 1969.

These costumed gentlemen are about to take part in the City of Canterbury's civic celebrations for the Coronation of Elizabeth II. This took the form of an elaborate historical pageant along the city wall rampart in Dane John and took place on the evenings of Tuesday 2 and Wednesday 3 June 1953. These characters are, from left to right: Ludyard, Becket, Ethelbert and Augustine, together with assorted monks and knights.

Another informal pose of characters about to appear in the city's official Coronation celebration pageant. These four proud ladies are arranged in Queen Victoria's pony chaise in the Dane John. Victoria of course, is the woman dressed in black (far left). Her royal companions are: Queen Bertha, Joan the fair maid of Kent, and Katherine of Aragon. The theme of the pageant was Canterbury's long association with the Crown, with characters enacting events from the city's historical past.

The stage is set for the start of the pageant along the top of the city wall. The expectant audience are gathered in the moat below, waiting for the first character to appear. The loudspeaker in the birch tree relayed music for community singing, which took place before the pageant and also broadcast a speech transmitted from London by the Prime Minister, Sir Winston Churchill. The heraldic coats of arms, fixed to the city wall and bastions, were painted by the College of Art.

The first group of characters in the Coronation pageant, which began at 9.10 p.m. make their way along the city wall rampart. The Emperor, Septimus Severus, looks down onto the crowd in the moat below, whilst his two sons, Geta and Caracalla, follow behind on horseback. In AD 206, the real Septimus Severus visited Canterbury to inspect the construction work on the new city wall circuit. Today, much of the Roman work still survives in the core of the wall, hidden beneath later work.

The next section of the pageant re-enacted the momentous events of AD 597. This was the year that Augustine, as the emissary of Pope Gregory, came to bring Christianity to England. With his entourage of monks (although there appear to be more nuns in the picture), he went to meet Ethelbert, the King of Kent. In fact, Christianity was already being practised on a small scale in Canterbury. Ethelbert's Queen, Bertha, worshipped daily in St Martin's Church.

The re-enactment of the martyrdom of Archbishop Becket at the hands of four knights of King Henry II. This, the most significant event in the history of Canterbury, was being staged on a platform high up on the Dane John Mound and must have been visible for miles. The huge Coronation crown, erected around the mound's memorial, was lit up at night. Subsequent sections of the pageant involved Edward III, Henry VIII, Queen Elizabeth, Charles II and Queen Victoria.

Four
New Developments
in the 1950s

Late September 1951, and the start of rebuilding activity on the north side of St George's Street. These workmen are actually carrying out the very first construction work of the Wilson Development Plan. This wall foundation for the new Woolworth's store is being laid in the cellar of a blitzed St George's Street building, thus effectively grafting the new city onto the ruins of the old one. The background is dominated by the Dean & Chapter's Burgate House development on the north side of Burgate Street (see overleaf).

The Burgate House development that filled one of the Blitz voids on the north side of Burgate Street. Begun in late 1950, it was the first post-war shopping development in the city centre. The entire north side of Burgate belongs to the Cathedral Dean & Chapter and, therefore, this development was not part of the Wilson Plan. Nor did the city architects department have much say in the architectural style adopted here. Consequently, what emerged was a building strongly influenced by the styles of the past, complete with dummy chimney stacks.

The Simon Langton Girls' School was the first major new building to be constructed in Canterbury after the Second World War, even pre-dating the Wilson Plan. Work began in 1948 and was completed by early 1951. The site chosen for the new development was the girls school's existing playing fields off Old Dover Road. Designed by City architect Hugh Wilson, the style of the building owes much more to the Art Deco or International movement of the 1930s, than the modernist, contemporary styles soon to appear in central Canterbury.

The first newly completed terrace of houses at numbers 1 to 10 Knight Avenue, at the beginning of the new London Road Estate, pictured on 15 March 1952. Initially, the estate was to be called New Harbledown, but boundary changes brought the new development into the city and the name was dropped. By this time, most if not all of the new tenants had already moved in and were beginning to tend their front gardens. Note the complete absence of parked cars, telephone lines and television aerials, all of which were expensive luxuries at this time.

This group includes all of the men who were responsible for the early post-war rebuilding of Canterbury. The photograph was taken in 1952, outside No. 27 Squire Avenue, on the occasion of the visit by Ernest Marples, MP (centre) from the Ministry of Housing and Local Government. Left to right, they are: Councillor Barrett, Chairman of the City Planning Committee; the Mayor Stanley Jennings; Ernest Marples, MP; City Architect Hugh Wilson; Canon De Laubanque; and Town Clark, John Boyle.

The new Woolworth shop on the north side of St George's Street, on 24 July 1952, a day before opening. However, its window displays had already attracted the attention of passers by. This was the first new development in post-war St George's Street – a thoroughfare all but obliterated in the Blitz (see page 6). The Woolworth's building, with its flat roof and brick elevations over a steel frame, heralded a type of construction that was to be repeated in many new buildings throughout the early and mid 1950s.

Friday 25 January 1952: a massive queue had formed outside Woolworth's, everyone eagerly waiting for the doors to be opened. My grandmother Crampton was in the queue that day and she used to tell a very amusing story about it. Apparently, when the doors finally opened, the whole queue surged forward as one. She remembers being carried around the inside of the shop by the sheer weight of numbers, barely able to put her feet on the ground, let alone stop to look at or buy anything! Distant and on the far side of Iron Bar Lane, the side elevation for the new Dolcis premises is taking shape.

The recently completed showroom premises for the South Eastern Gas Board, on the corner of Best Lane and the High Street. The more traditional style of this building is very similar to those depicted by Dr Charles Holden in the drawings for his abandoned 1945 development plan. The new shop's position, set well back from the existing street lines, clearly indicates that the widening of Best Lane – and even the High Street approaches to the Kings Bridge – were planned for later.

The newly finished headquarters for the *Kentish Gazette*, on the north side of St George's Place, in March 1954. This has also been set well back to allow for the dualling of St George's Place, which finally took place in 1969. This area was part of the thirty-four acres of compulsory purchase required for the first stage of the Wilson Plan and designated for light industrial and office use. However, by late 1954, the plan had run into financial trouble and the city council were already turning away from the idea of compulsory purchase for the continuance of the development plan.

The first phase of the colonnaded terrace of shops on the south side of St George's Street, the building of which was completed in early 1953. By January 1954, when this picture was taken, every unit had been occupied. A new service road had been created behind the shops with access from St George's Lane. A foot passage, locally known as Whitefriars Passage, passed through this development to give access to the Simon Langton Boys' School beyond. The passage continued in use after the school was closed in 1959 (see page 69).

The premises of grocers David Greig, on the corner of St George's Street and Canterbury Lane, was one of the most radically designed, modernist developments in post-war Canterbury. Designed by Robert Paine & Partners and completed in 1953, it shows the influence of architecture as demonstrated at the 1951 London Festival of Britain. In 1956, the development was awarded an RIBA bronze medal. Recently fully restored, it is one of the few modernist buildings likely to escape the city council's current demolition purge.

The finishing touches being applied to the new Cathedral Library in 1953. Designed by architect John Denman in a pastiche of older styles, the new building was a replacement for the library which received a direct hit in the June 1942 Blitz of Canterbury. Like its Victorian predecessor, the new library was being built onto, and incorporated the remains of Archbishop Lanfranc's eleventh-century dormitory. The new building was officially opened on 18 July 1954.

Archbishop Geoffrey Fisher officially opens the new Diocesan House in the summer of 1955. The building was constructed on a large corner plot between Lady Wootton's Green and Broad Street. The site was once occupied by an old house, which had associations with Charles Dickens. Sadly, it was demolished in 1942, following Blitz damage. As with all other new Dean and Chapter buildings such as Burgate House and the Cathedral Library, Diocesan House was designed in a safe neo-Georgian style that shunned the modernism of the city council's developments.

The stunning National Westminster Bank, on the corner of the Longmarket and St George's Street, as new in July 1956. Surely one of the city's finest early post-war buildings, its construction incorporated quality materials such as Portland stone, slate and bricks. The interior boasted a large and impressive mural. Regrettably, despite its architectural superiority (a fact acknowledged by English Heritage) and public appeals by the author, it was demolished in 1996 and replaced by over-scale pastiche fakery. The demise of such a fine building proves that official ignorance and short-sightedness is, sadly, not a thing of the past.

The St George's Clock tower development in 1955; a brave attempt to amalgamate the old with the new. The terrace of shops, centre and left, were built by Ravenseft, who were also responsible for the earlier colonnaded terrace of shops on the south side of St George's Street. This view makes an interesting comparison to the late 1940s photograph on page 16, taken from the same spot. This clock tower development perished in 1990 and, after an extensive archaeological investigation, was replaced by a much denser scheme.

The Mayor, Alderman W.S. Bean, together with his officials and a management team from the East Kent Road Car Company, survey the new bus station off St George's Lane, in October 1956. Just seen furthest right is the old Simon Langton School buildings, which until their demolition in 1960, directly abutted the bus station (see page 69). The office building, from which the scene is being surveyed, was demolished in late 1999 as part of the Whitefriars development project. Its replacement by two buildings in a post-modernist style, is a refreshing change from the recent plethora of pastiche.

Marlowe House, on the north side of St George's Street and opposite the junction with St George's Lane, March 1957. It was built immediately east of the clock tower development seen on page 44. New occupants the Co-op later extended the building at the rear and along the frontage of Burgate Lane. C & A later traded here for many years, but at the time of writing, the building was being adapted for new owners Wilkinsons. Its escape from demolition and replacement by a tourist pleasing 'Disneyland' development, is to be welcomed.

An impressive display of period hats and spectacles, at the opening ceremony for the new Frank Hooker Secondary School complex, in July 1956. The need for a new secondary school off London Road Estate, as well as that of the adjacent Beauherne Primary School, was identified in the Wilson Plan. Two other secondary modern schools for Canterbury were planned and these later appeared as the Archbishop's and St Anselm's schools.

The premises of Hallett's filling station and Ford motor dealership, in September 1957. It is situated in the extra-mural suburb of St Dunstan's at the junction of St Dunstan's Street and Station Road West. It is interesting to observe the contrasting styles of their original early 1950s 'Holdenesque' neo-Georgian building (right), with the flat roofed modernist extension recently completed to the left. Both buildings are now completely obscured behind a massive forecourt canopy.

The smart new modernist Sun Building, between St George's Terrace (left) and St George's Lane, nearing completion in December 1957. It was built on an overgrown site, once occupied by the previous Sun building, destroyed in the Baedeker raid on Canterbury of 1 June 1942. Between then and the construction of their new premises, the Sun Insurance Company operated from offices at No. 1 Castle Street. The new Sun Building was pulled down exactly forty-two years after its construction as part of the Whitefriars Scheme.

Two schoolboys observe the all-male gathering for the official opening of the new Nag's Head public house in Dover Street, during March 1958. This is the fourth version of the Nag's Head to occupy the same site. The original pub, in a collection of seventeenth and eighteenth-century buildings on the street frontage, was replaced by a purpose-built neo-Georgian pub, set well back, in 1931. This second version was blitzed in 1942 and replaced by a temporary pre-fabricated building, which lasted until its permanent replacement in 1958.

Building in progress on a row of single-storey shop units on the east side of Iron Bar Lane, in November 1958. In general, the new developments of the late 1950s under the auspices of Canterbury City Council were much more austere and architecturally far less successful than their early 1950s counterparts. Financial difficulties were a major contributory factor. The single terrace is due for demolition in 2002 and replacement by a 'theme park' pastiche development, demanding much higher rents, is threatened.

New buildings on the east side of the Longmarket, nearing completion in around January 1959. At the far end in St George's Street the National Provincial Bank, discussed earlier this chapter, can be seen. In the foreground, a pile of rubble is all that is left of the recently demolished Regency period Corn Exchange gateway (see page 24). The pre-fabricated shops to the right – also featured earlier – would be dismantled in late 1959 and replaced by an ambitious and controversial modernist development (see page 89).

Five
Scenes from the 1950s

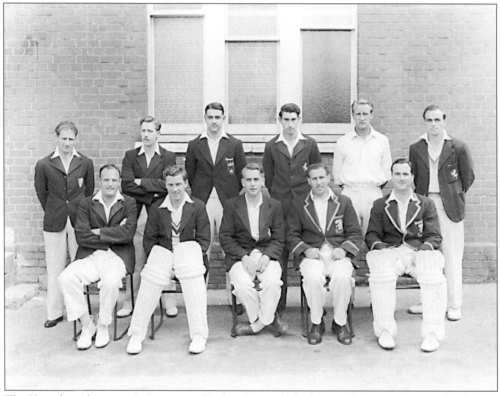

The Kent first eleven at St Lawrence Cricket Ground, the home of Kent cricket, on 10 August 1951. Based on the Kent first innings, they are, from left to right: A.E. Fagg, A.H. Phebey, P. Hearn, M.C. Cowdrey, B.R. Edrich, R. Mayes, D.G. Clark, G. Evans, R.R. Dovey, D.V.P. Wright, F. Ridgeway. Undoubtedly, the most famous of these gentlemen is Colin Cowdrey, who went on to become captain of both Kent and England.

A queue waits in the chilly January air for the Baldwin's Winter Sale to open. Baldwin's was one of the larger and most popular department stores in early post-war Canterbury (see page 33). Just to the right of the shop is the County Hotel, which has changed very little in the intervening years. Baldwin's itself closed in the late 1960s and the old building demolished, to be replaced by two modern shop units.

Canterbury's carnival queen for 1953, seventeen-year-old Sylvia Sackett (the blonde-haired girl left of centre), stands amongst the members of the carnival committee. Standing to her right is Mrs Vie Chappell who, at the time, ran the White Swan Restaurant in Northgate. Her daughter Wendy, who is standing at the front of the group, presented the bouquet to Miss Sackett. Today, interest in becoming the carnival queen has declined and no longer has the glamour it once had in the 1950s.

A group of smiling children and adults watch firemen demonstrate the use of a turntable ladder. The scene is from April 1953, during the Canterbury fire station open day. At the time, the fire station was situated at the former St Lawrence Farm site along Old Dover Road. The converted farmhouse can be seen behind, as can the city's famous 1939 fire engine, AJG500. A new purpose-built station would be constructed in Upper Bridge Street during the mid-1960s (see page 95).

The Kent Miners May Day parade passing through the Westgate and into St Peter's Street, during May 1953. At this time, the Kent coalfield consisted of four very productive pits at Chislet, Snowdown, Tilmanstone and Bettshanger. Sadly, they are no more, as much a victim of politics as they were the decline in the demand for coal. Also negotiating the Westgate is double-decker EFN 190, an East Kent Guy Arab bus of 1950, once a common sight on the streets of Canterbury.

A small section of the huge crowd on the north side of St Dunstan's Street, eagerly awaiting the start of Canterbury Carnival in the summer of 1953. Many of the adults are straining to see the first float turn out of nearby Roper Road to their right, although most of the children seem more interested in the photographer. Note the coach-built prams at the front, in an age before the buggy was invented. The empty site behind would finally be developed with the arrival of the National Tyre Service garage in the early 1970s.

During the early 1950s, the Cathedral's ancient and precious stained glass was finally restored to its rightful place. It had been removed and stored in the crypt's St Gabriel's Chapel since 1938, when hostilities seemed likely. This task was undertaken by the cathedral's master glazier, Samuel Caldwell (right), who was around one hundred years old when this picture was taken. The man holding the stained glass panel is his assistant George Easton. Sam, who was an older brother of Rupert Bear's creator Mary Tourtel, died in 1954, aged 102!

The cast of the pantomime *Mother Goose*, from the Sydney Woodman School of Dancing, pose for the camera in January 1954. The venue is the Garrison Theatre in Military Road. The goose was played by Annette Potter, now Annette Boorman. She says that the costume was uncomfortable and extremely hot! At the end of the show, there was a ditty always quoted, along the lines of, 'And now the goose gets hotter and hotter, let's lift the head and see Annette Potter!'

The excited group of children – interspersed with a few adults – is the 1953 Christmas outing from the Cherry Tree pub in Whitehorse Lane. They are about to head around to nearby St Margaret's Street and the Marlowe Theatre, to see the pantomime. Members of the Sayer, Crunden, Harris, Marsh, Hinders and Daniels families can be seen amongst them. At the time, there were a number of houses in Whitehorse Lane and the adjoining Jewry Lane, making up quite a little community.

A spectacular blaze rips through the roof of the partly timber-framed three-storey premises of Court Brothers (Furnishers) Ltd, on the corner of Burgate and Butchery Lane, during the first week of January 1955. Six fire appliances from Canterbury, Chilham, Wingham and Sturry took the best part of an hour to get the fire under control. Ironically, this building had survived the conflagration of the June 1942 Blitz, which had destroyed its immediate neighbours. Afterwards, the upper storeys were demolished, but the ground floor portion continued to trade until 1959 (see page 26).

A Boy Scouts' St George's Day Parade traverses St George's Crossroads, April 1955. Behind are two buildings, no longer part of today's cityscape and destined to be pulled down for St George's Roundabout and the second stage of the ring road (see page 117). Far right is part of the Co-op premises, a former theatre that disappeared in 1961 (see page 73). In the centre is tobacconist & confectioner Pettit & Son, which hung on until 1969 and was pulled down just prior to the making of the roundabout (see page 116).

The now homeless occupants of numbers 19 and 20 New Town Street, Mrs Payne and Mr and Mrs Michael Palmer, standing forlornly outside the ruins of their homes, in November 1955. The early Victorian cottages, situated at the end of a terrace that sloped down to the River Stour, were thought to have been the victims of subsidence. Fortunately, their sudden collapse resulted in no one being seriously hurt. Further subsidence in the 1960s resulted in the demolition of the entire terrace.

A 1957 view of the High Street section of Canterbury's main street, near its junction with Guildhall Street (right). Buses and bicycles predominate; a scene that today's environmental lobby would greatly envy! The double-decker in the foreground is about to complete its journey from Margate. Only a year before, it would have turned right at the Guildhall Street Junction instead of left as it does now, to head for the old bus station in St Peter's Place. The K shoe shop on the corner, had recently replaced the last remains of the old Guildhall (see page 17).

Children from the Kingsmead Primary School inspect the construction of their new swimming pool, May 1959. The school itself, which is accessed from St John's Place, is on the right. The late Georgian terraced houses beyond the flint wall are in St Radigund's Place, which is a turning off Duck Lane (see page 77). The houses would be pulled down in the mid-1960s, ostensibly to free the site for the ring road – stage three – and the proposed Sturry 'Radial' road; the latter being an A28 bypass. In the event, both road plans were scrapped.

A Salvation Army parade passes along Stour Street and makes its way towards the army headquarters in nearby Whitehorse Lane, October 1957. The participants seem more interested in the *Kentish Gazette* photographer than they are in their senior officers, who are standing on the raised platform in front of the Poor Priests Hospital (right). Behind are the truncated remains of Beasley & Son Dry Cleaners, who lost much of their front building in the June 1942 Blitz. The site would be redeveloped in the 1960s.

A dramatic scene just off the level crossing in St Dunstan's Street, during November 1958. One carriage of a train leaving Canterbury West station had become derailed. The station itself is just visible in the background. On the left, a steam crane summoned from Ashford, is about to move into position and lift the errant coach back onto the rails. On the right, a temporarily marooned tank engine blows off steam. Today, the track layout at the west station has been considerably reduced, including the elimination of the central through tracks.

Another scene of a Boy Scouts' St George's Day Parade, this one captured in Broad Street, in April 1959. Note the clandestine nose-picker, bottom right! What is probably of more interest is the pair of cottages beyond at numbers 2 and 3 Broad Street. At this time, No. 2 was the home of Mrs Goldup and it is probably her who has come outside to watch the parade. Number three was empty. The gaps either side were caused by the raids of 1942. Both cottages would be demolished in the 1960s.

The beginning of the reconstruction of St George's Street in the spring of 1952. The Woolworth's shop is nearing completion, whilst on the left, a sign announces that the construction of new premises for the Dolcis Shoe Company, and James Walker Jeweller was about to begin. A utility bodied Guy Arab East Kent bus heads westwards on the 27a service from Thannington to Blean. The narrowness of St George's Street is quite apparent, with the bus occupying most of the available width. Street widening would begin in October 1952.

By the end of the 1950s, the redevelopment of St George's Street was all but complete, as this view clearly testifies. Woolworth's is now only one of a number of individually built shopping developments on the north side of the street. Nearest the camera is the front elevation of the much-missed National Provincial Bank building (see page 44). St George's Street itself has by now been considerably widened, enough to allow on-street parking on the south side and with plenty of room for the bus to pass by. At the far end, the restored St George's Clock tower has become a familiar landmark.

Six

The Ring Road
Stage One

A notice just off the old London Road proudly proclaims that the construction of Canterbury's ring road had begun. Talk of a ring road had begun as early as the 1920s, when tentative moves were made to acquire land for its construction. Then, in the early 1930s, part of Broad Street was widened, following the demolition of the Starr Brewery. The rival early post-war development plans all included a completed ring road, although there was much disagreement about the route it should take.

Officials gather amongst the heavy plant for a ceremony to mark the beginning of work for the new road, on 29 March 1962. Cllr George Briscall, chairman of the council's highways committee, performed the official 'turning of the first sod' ceremony, but used a mechanical excavator rather than the usual silver spade. Around a mile of new dual-carriageway was proposed for stage one, to run from the junction of London Road and Knight Avenue to Wincheap Green, via a roundabout at the top of St Peter's Place.

An October 1962 view of work in progress, as seen from Knight Avenue. The notice featured in the first picture is on the far left. The road works are for the A2 diversion and ring road, two of Kent's major trunk routes which crossed in the middle of the city at the time, and caused much congestion. Moreover, the existing A2 route at the time had to negotiate the bottlenecks of the St Dunstan's level crossing and the Westgate towers. Thus, the new road would serve both purposes and allow the A2 and A28 traffic to meet at the proposed Wincheap Green Roundabout.

The Cementation Co Ltd construct the buttresses for a bridge that will carry the new road over the Ashford to Ramsgate railway, in the late summer of 1962. In total, four over-bridges would be needed, the other three being for Whitehall Road and both branches of the River Stour. A brand new 4-CEP electric train glides past on an Ashford-bound service. Steam working had been abandoned on this line only months before (see page 83). A redundant signal box can be seen beyond the new bridge. Its brick base is still evident today.

Girders for the River Stour Bridge at the top end of the Westgate Gardens, being lowered into place at the beginning of July 1962. The bridge girders were constructed at Norwich and brought to Canterbury West, where a lorry with a 45ft trailer took them, one at a time, to the construction site. The total cost for the new road was estimated at £694,973 – the vast majority of which was covered by a grant from the Ministry of Transport.

The empty houses of numbers 1 to 8 Camden Terrace at the top end of St Peter's Place in 1961. Built in the 1880s, their sturdy Victorian brick construction contrasted with the stuccoed Regency artisan terraced houses to be found in the remainder of St Peter's Place, which dated from the 1830s. Ironically, it was these more recent properties that were about to be demolished for the St Peter's roundabout. This proposed roundabout would link the purely A2 diversion part of the new dual carriageway with the actual ring road section from St Peter's Place to Wincheap Green.

Late 1962, and Camden Terrace has given way to St Peter's Roundabout, which can be seen being laid out in the middle distance. Beyond, surviving buildings in St Peter's Place can be seen, including the Holy Cross School, centre right (see page 106), which would be demolished in the 1970s. In the foreground, the St Peter's Place to Wincheap Green portion of the new dual carriageway is taking shape. At this point, the new road crosses the line of the old city wall, of which there was no trace remaining in this part of the city.

An early 1960s view across the River Stour, towards the terraced houses of Wincheap Grove and other properties around Wincheap Green beyond. In the foreground, a man sows seed in the well-prepared soil of one of the tannery allotments. Left of centre is the flint walled former vicarage once associated with the nearby St Mildred's Church. To the right, the more prominent terrace of houses is numbers 26 to 45 Wincheap Green, also known as Meadow Cottages.

A similar view to the one above, dating from late summer 1962, by which time, Wincheap Grove had gone and construction of the ring road was well advanced. The last of the four bridges needed was already in place across the River Stour. Beyond, men prepare the soil of a vast embankment, where once others tended their allotments. The vast amount of earth needed for this embankment was excavated from the redundant Elham Valley railway embankment running through nearby Wincheap. It was then transported here by the lorry load.

The terraced houses of Wincheap Grove, with the allotments and River Stour accessible through the gates at the end of the street. The mainly nineteenth-century terrace, known as Meadow Cottages (seen earlier) is on the left. To the right is the junction for Church Lane St Mildred's, which connects through to Stour Street. Beyond the junction, the unpainted rendered building is the former Foresters Arms public house. It had closed many years before and been converted into two cottages.

An April 1961 view of the top end of Wincheap Grove from its junction with Castle Street. Note the steep slope in this part of the lane, which partly explains why a huge earth embankment would be needed at this location once work on the ring road began. On the right is the end of a terrace fronting Castle Street, soon to be demolished. Part way down Wincheap Grove, the rendered cottages of numbers 1 to 15 are already roofless and stripped out in preparation for their demolition. At the far end of the lane, Meadow Cottages have already been pulled down.

The Wincheap Green area, *c.* 1960, looking north along Castle Street from the East station railway embankment. In the foreground, Wincheap Street curves in from the left to become Wincheap Green briefly, then Pin Hill. Furthest left is the headquarters of the British Road Services Ltd, followed by the junction for Wincheap Grove. Beyond is the terrace at numbers 32 to 36 Castle Street, part of which was visible in the previous picture. Opposite and on the corner between Castle Street and Wincheap Green is the Castle Hotel and public house.

Another view of the Wincheap Green area, this time looking east along Wincheap Green itself, which soon becomes Pin Hill. The picture is dominated by the impressive red-bricked St Andrew's Presbyterian Church. It was designed by City Architect John Green Hall and built in 1880. Furthest right is the curved façade of the Station Hotel, which would later become the Man of Kent. This area was about to be radically altered by the construction of the Wincheap Green roundabout. Many of the buildings featured in the top picture would perish but – for now – St Andrew's Church would remain intact (see page 123).

Wincheap Green looking west towards Wincheap Street, from the point where it becomes Pin Hill. Far left is the side elevation of St Andrew's Presbyterian Church. On the right are the few properties of Wincheap Green, dominated by the double-fronted detached house at No. 3, which was, by now, standing empty. Further from the camera are the single-storey premises of A.T. Friend, wholesale newsagent (No. 2), followed by R. & V. Green's transport café at No. 1 Wincheap Green. The Castle Hotel is at the far end of the group.

By January 1963, demolition work in advance of the construction of Wincheap roundabout had already begun. Little remained of the large detached house at No. 3 Wincheap Green. A.T. Friend now appears to be closed, but the presence of the parked lorries means that Green's transport café is still open, at least for now. Furthest right, is the now familiar façade of the old Sessions House in Castle Street, revealed following the clearance for the roundabout.

The top end of Wincheap Street in early 1961, looking south from the junction of Wincheap Grove (far right) and with Castle Street behind the camera. On the right is the impressive office of B.R.S. Ltd, in a large Georgian house once known as The Cedars. Prior to nationalisation in 1949, these were the premises of local hauliers C. & G. Yeoman. To the left are the properties at numbers 1 to 7 Wincheap Street (in the old numbering sequence). Number 1, nearer the camera, is a double-fronted stuccoed property and the home of Walter Yeoman.

By the spring of 1963, Wincheap roundabout was in place, but there remained a considerable amount of tidying up to do. The B.R.S. building, together with numbers 1 and 2 Wincheap Street, had already been pulled down to make way for the new roundabout. Numbers 3 to 7, seen here, were all to have been retained. However, the discovery of dry rot in the fabric of No. 3 – nearest the camera – sealed its fate and it was demolished shortly after this picture was taken.

Canterbury's Mayor, Councillor E.E. Kingsman (left) extends the hand of friendship towards the Mayor of Rheims, Monsieur Tattinger, during the opening ceremony for the new dual carriageway, in June 1963. Earlier, in May 1962, Canterbury had twinned with the French cathedral city of Rheims. Therefore, it seemed only fitting that a delegation from our twinned city be invited to the opening ceremony for the new road and for that road to be named 'Rheims Way'.

A pair of East Kent coaches tours the route of the new Rheims Way, following an official welcoming ceremony for the Rheims delegation at the Cathedral's Chapter House. The new road instantly transformed the traffic situation in Canterbury and put pressure on the council to complete the ring road. In actual fact, the Rheims Way accounted for only 20% of the proposed ring road circuit. The ring road's second stage, a further 30%, would not be completed until 1969 (see chapter 11).

Seven
Demolition in the 1960s

Part of the Simon Langton Boys' School complex on the Whitefriars site, in the summer of 1959. The triple gabled block was built in 1914 and comprised classrooms 15, 16 and 17 on the first floor, with the school's gymnasium below. The boys' school relocated to new buildings at Nackington in November 1959, with the old Whitefriars buildings being demolished in the summer of 1960. The site of the 1914 block was used for the dualling of St George's Lane in 1962. Much of the playground area in the foreground was taken up by the widening of Gravel Walk in the same year.

August 1960 – a tower-like structure being demolished at Canterbury Gas Works, which could once be found towards the top end of Castle Street. Note the man balancing on the remaining wall of the structure, in an age before the Health and Safety at Work Act! The gas works tower, which was visible for miles from the south west approaches to the city, had only been built in the last few decades and was already redundant. The city gas works were situated right next to Canterbury Castle and the ruins of the keep had been used to store coal for the works as recently as the 1920s.

An interesting study of a row of late Georgian buildings, on the west side of Wincheap Street in the summer of 1962. Far left, is the narrow junction for Simmonds Row. To its right is the former Pilgrim's Cycles shop at numbers 17 and 18 which had been badly damaged by fire in April of the same year. Fire damage is also evident in the roof of the adjacent empty house. The former shops of L. Preen (number 15) and the delicatessen at number 14, are also derelict. The entire terrace had gone by 1964. Later, Simmonds Row was widened to become the access road to Wincheap Industrial Estate.

The rear elevations of numbers 16 and 17 Old Ruttington Lane, one of a number of pre-slum clearance reference photographs taken in the late 1950s and early 1960s. Far right, Mr Thomas Lewis stands in the back yard of his threatened home. Number 17 (left) was the dwelling of Mr Abdul Karim. At No. 15, off camera to the right, the occupant was Miss Cook. Following the demolition of numbers 15 to 17, the site was used to expand the grounds of the adjacent St Thomas' Roman Catholic School.

Numbers 38 to 42 Old Ruttington Lane, standing empty in October 1961. The lane, of early medieval origin, once ran around the northern and eastern sides of the extra-mural precincts for St Gregory's Priory, founded by Lanfranc in the 1080s. Following the demolition of the last of the priory buildings in the early 1800s, the entire precinct area was developed with terraced houses, largely for the families of soldiers stationed at the nearby barracks. By the early 1960s, the vast majority of those houses were included in a massive slum clearance scheme.

Live demolition in progress on the east side of Military Road, in December 1961. The end wall of No. 77 comes crashing to the ground, whilst a workman (far right) runs for his life! Military Road was once one of a number of new thoroughfares laid out across the former St Gregory's Priory precincts, to serve the nearby barracks. Following the clearance, much of the road's east side was used once more to expand the grounds for St Thomas' School as well as to provide a site for the new ambulance station (see page 94).

A fascinating interim view looking across Union Street and towards the Cathedral, in early 1962. Union Street was another of the new roads constructed in the early 1800s, as mentioned above. It was taken from one of a development of new houses and flats, recently built on the street's north side, following slum clearance (see page 28). The late Georgian terrace on the south side stands forlornly stripped of all re-useable parts, prior to demolition. Just left of centre is the former Union Castle public house, its last orders having long since been called (see page 93).

The old Co-operative store at numbers 11 and 12 Lower Bridge Street, standing empty and awaiting demolition in April 1961. It stood at St George's Crossroads, on the corner between Lower Bridge Street and St George's Gate, which was soon to become a roundabout. This work would be part of the second stage of the ring road, which would not get under way until 1969 (see chapter 11). By 1961, the Co-op had relocated to their new shop behind, which had recently been greatly extended (see page 45).

The Rose Lane elevation of the premises of greengrocers H.S. Brewer & Son, February 1962. The shop stood on the west corner of Rose Lane with Watling Street and was numbered 15a in the latter street's sequence. The property's stuccoed Regency period façade may have hidden an older structure. The crumbling wall to the right is early seventeeth century and is associated with the Jacobean period house still surviving in Watling Street today. Brewer's was pulled down in the same year to widen Rose Lane (see page 125).

A superb piece of lost quality cityscape, on the west side of King Street. Nearest the camera is the former Eight Bells public house (No. 43), which by now had become the Amos & Dawton auction rooms. At the far end is the Prince of Wales pub at No. 51. Both pub buildings survive today, but everything between has gone. The triple-jettied gables of numbers 44 and 45 are typical of Canterbury vernacular architecture of the late seventeenth century. These gorgeous properties had gone by 1961. The rest of the terrace perished in 1962.

A contrast between ancient and modern in Upper Bridge Street, during 1964. In the foreground is the rear of the early nineteenth-century single-storey Harris' Almshouses, being stripped prior to demolition. They were numbered 12 to 17 Upper Bridge Street and until recently, had been occupied by single or widowed ladies. The site was being cleared for the Lombard House office development (see page 96). Soaring up behind and more dominant than the Cathedral's Bell Harry Tower, is the Riceman's department store in St George's Lane, which was by now two years old (see page 92).

A small crowd watch a fire being put out in a derelict building on the south side of Gravel Walk. Until recently, this structure (at No. 6 Gravel Walk) had been used by W.S. Williams & Son, coach builders, as a paint store. The blaze occurred on 1 April 1964, and was no joke for the firemen who had to contend with the fiercely burning cans of paint stored in the old building. The north side of Gravel Walk had been demolished in 1960 for road widening. The buildings on the south side would perish in 1965.

A charming mid-seventeenth century house in Whitehorse Lane, which would be cherished today, but in June 1965 was derelict and awaiting demolition. For many years, the old property was the premises of George Snell, Printer (at numbers 5 and 5a). To the right is a pair of late eighteenth century cottages at numbers six and seven. Within months, all three buildings would be pulled down for road widening. This would then allow Whitehorse Lane to become a link road between the existing main street and the proposed cross-city relief road further to the south. None of these road plans were ever fulfilled, despite much advance clearance.

Demolition in progress – of three substantial kilns situated at the former quarry and lime works of Frank Cooper Ltd, in September 1965. Demand for lime by the building trade had considerably tailed off in the early post-war years, and the company finally closed in 1964. The pulling down of these lime kilns proved to be more difficult than anticipated. Their continued use at high temperatures for over thirty years had hardened the brickwork into a solid mass. However, cracks in the kiln furthest right, show that progress was finally being made.

A young couple walk past the shabby façade of the Freemasons Tavern in St Margaret's Street, during April 1965. The pub's lop-sided nature and partially corrugated iron roof, are due to the fact that half of the structure was lost in the June 1942 Blitz. Now, the remaining portion was due to be pulled down to make way for the new relief road that was planned to cross the city, east to west, just south of the existing main street. Despite the demise of the Freemasons Tavern and numerous other properties, the proposed road was never completed.

The early nineteenth-century terraced houses on the north-west side of St Radigund's Place, May 1966. By this time, many of the properties were standing empty. However, still resident at No. 6 in the shadow of the sycamore sapling, was Miss O. Emery and, further left at No. 4, Mr David Gebbie. Ostensibly to be pulled down as part of a slum clearance programme, the house's demolition would also free the site for the proposed third stage of the ring road and A28 relief road to Sturry (see page 56). Following the cancellation of both schemes, much of the cleared St Radigund's area became a hotch potch of little car parks.

Early post-war prefabricated houses being dismantled, just off New Dover Road and to the east of Canterbury, in February 1967. Commonly known as 'pre-fabs', they were a popular sight around the outskirts of the city for over twenty years. Most were erected in small estates with concrete roads, wherever there was vacant land at the outer limits of the existing built up area. Each individual estate had roads and passages named after a theme. Those seen here commemorated British wartime leaders: Churchill Road, Montgomery, Alexander, Mountbatten, Cunningham, and Harris Avenues.

The rarely photographed houses of St Stephen's Fields, viewed from the upper storey of an adjacent property, c. 1966. St Stephen's Fields were a curious L-shaped block of properties that appeared to date from the early to mid-nineteenth century, although the projecting white painted property nearest the camera is of a later date. Some of the houses were already empty by 1960. All would be pulled down shortly after this picture was taken. Far left is part of the works for Barretts of Canterbury Ltd. This too is now but a memory.

A fascinating mixture of terraced houses, ranging from the seventeenth to the twentieth centuries, at the top end of Northgate in July 1966. Many properties had already gone, including much of the street's west side (left) and a pair of cottages, where the dust cart is parked. The latter had given way for the new premises of Bishop's Taxis. Everything in this view – with the exception of the most distant properties – has since been demolished. Today, the street's east side (right) is dominated by the tall red-brick Northgate House office development (see page 107).

The top end of Castle Street in the spring of 1968, dominated by the substantial Victorian brick buildings of the former gas works. Some of their redundant buildings had been pulled down in 1960 (see page 70). Now, only the offices of the Canterbury & District Water Co., remained open on the site. The land had recently been purchased by Canterbury City Council and all the remaining buildings, including a gasometer (just out of sight to the left) would be demolished. A massive temporary surface car park would then be created (see page 128).

The white painted former Princess Charlotte public house, at the foot of St Martin's Hill, just prior to demolition in March 1967. The adjacent boarded-up terraced houses at numbers 4 to 10 St Martin's Hill, were also about to go. The houses were compulsorily purchased as slums under the 1957 Housing Act. In the 1960s, if properties were in the way of a road-building, or as in this case, widening scheme, it was easier and cheaper for the city council to have them declared as unfit for human habitation. Less money could then be paid to the hapless owners.

The charming and unique house at No. 7 Artillery Gardens, as seen in 1968. One could almost imagine this cottage with its lush garden, being in a tiny village, were it not for the roofs and chimneys of Artillery Street (left) and Artillery Gardens on the right. All these properties were part of the Northgate Barracks development of the early nineteenth century, discussed earlier in this chapter. The so-called slum clearance schemes of the 1960s were always completely inclusive and soon, No. 7 would be demolished along with its terraced neighbours.

A rear view of the High Street premises of drapers and outfitters Baldwin & Son, in 1969. (Images of the shop front can be found on pages 33 and 50.) As mentioned earlier, the rear elevation of many of Canterbury's buildings gives away their true age. Baldwin's was no exception. What we have here are two substantial medieval timber-framed buildings. The one on the left has a gable end, whereas, the most probably older property on the right has a hipped roof and adjoining staircase turret. Incredibly, all would soon be pulled down for an extension to the adjacent County Hotel and two shop units.

Eight

Transport

The last train from Whitstable Harbour whistles as it pulls off the branch line and enters Canterbury West station, on Saturday 29 November 1952. The old Canterbury to Whitstable line, affectionately known as the Crab & Winkle, had opened as early as 1830. It once boasted of possessing the oldest railway bridge in the world. Competition from buses in the early 1930s had led to the withdrawl of passenger services on the line. Similarly, it was the emergence of modern lorries in the early 1950s that caused the loss of the freight business and brought about the closure of the line.

A Bulleid-designed Pacific steam locomotive of the Battle of Britain class pauses by the water crane at Canterbury East station, on a stopping train for the coast in May 1959. This was during the last few weeks of steam operation on the line, with the electric 'third rail' for the new generation of trains, already installed. The locomotive of 1946, numbered 34070 and named *Manston*, was withdrawn from service in August 1964 and finally rescued for preservation, but only after languishing in Barry scrapyard for eighteen years.

The new order at Canterbury East station, in the shape of a newly built electric locomotive, number E5000. It glides through the station in May 1959, hauling a lengthy mixed freight train bound for Faversham Marshalling Yard. Later designated Class 71, these powerful locomotives were equally at home on passenger turns, regularly hauling the prestigious 'Golden Arrow' and 'Night Ferry' trains between Victoria and the south-east Kent coastal ports.

Members of the public examine examples of the new trains, marshalled in the coal yard sidings of the East station, in May 1959. Nearest the buffers is a British Railways-built diesel locomotive D5014, from 1958. Later to become Class 24, these type two diesels had only a brief stay on the southern region. When I was eighteen months old, my parents took me to see the new trains, although regrettably I do not remember anything about it.

A Brighton-built standard tank locomotive waits to depart from Canterbury West station, with an Ashford-bound stopping train, in 1961. The Ashford to Ramsgate line, via Canterbury West, hung onto its steam locomotives for two years more than the Faversham to Dover line, via Canterbury East, as seen opposite. Nevertheless, it too submitted to the efficient, yet silent and lifeless electric trains shortly after this picture was taken. Surviving steam operation on the Southern Region concentrated on the West Country routes, before finally ceasing in the summer of 1967.

A rank of rusty and derelict steam traction engines, being offered for scrap in Holman's Meadow, in 1951. The traction engines of local agricultural and general hauliers, Holman Brothers, were once a familiar sight on the streets of Canterbury as they trundled to and from the farms around the city. Beyond the engines is a new tractor – a symbol of the changed times and long since responsible for the old steam engine's downfall.

The 1953 carnival float from Invicta Motors parked in Lady Wootton's Green, prior to the Canterbury carnival of that year, for which they won third prize. The float contained a brand new Fordson tractor and bevy of 'Invicta Girls', proudly advertising the countries to which the company exported tractors. Of course, Miss Great Britain got to actually sit on the tractor! The same float also took part in Whitstable carnival that year and improved its tally by winning second prize.

A new East Kent double-decker parked outside the St Stephen's Road Garage in 1952, ready to undertake a tour of the Midlands. Its task was to promote the seaside holiday resorts of its native region. For the tour, the lower saloon seats were removed and an enquiry desk installed at the driver's end. The Guy Arab Mark II bus, EFN 362, lasted in service with the company until 1968. The St Stephen's depot was demolished in the mid-1990s.

Traffic chaos on the A2 at Dunkirk, October 1960, as the main road is blocked following a heavy collision. A coastal bound container lorry impacted with an East Kent double-decker on the No. 3 route from Canterbury to Faversham. The damage sustained by the AEC Regent Mark V, PFN 876, is clearly evident. Behind is the Gate Inn, a well-known pub and transport café. Now coupled with a filling station, the Gate Inn is on a slip road alongside the modern dualled A2 today.

Two East Kent buses edge past each other in St George's Street during October 1952, whilst traffic queues up behind. Further down the road, workmen are causing more delays. The early post-war rebuilding of St George's Street is well underway and hard core for road widening is being laid down, which greatly improved matters. According to the development plan, bus services would eventually use the proposed parallel relief road, discussed earlier. However, this was never built.

Another traffic bottleneck, further down the main street, was the Weavers or King's Bridge between High Street and St Peter's Street. This November 1954 view shows a utility built East Kent double-decker bus easing past what is probably an Austin A40 on the bridge. The aforementioned relief road would have solved the problem of this potential trouble-spot. It was planned to cross the Greyfriars Gardens, approximately one hundred yards south of the King's Bridge. Ultimately, the existing main road was pedestrianized.

Television, film and stage personality Jessie Matthews poses for the press at the wheel of a brand-new Ford Zephyr Convertible, during Invicta Motors' Service week, in April 1955. She joked with reporters that 'possession is nine points of the law', but was not allowed to keep the vehicle! The picture was taken at Invicta's garage premises in Lower Bridge Street. These were later greatly extended and rebuilt in the early 1960s (see page 90).

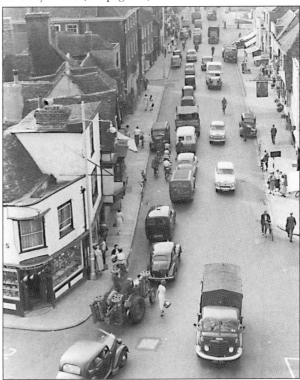

Rush hour traffic in St Dunstan's Street, as seen from the top of the Westgate, in August 1955. At the time, this was the main A2, carrying both through and local traffic. These vehicles not only had to contend with the King's Bridge bottleneck, but also the St Dunstan's railway level crossing, just visible at the top of the picture (see page 103). Eventually, the situation was eased by the opening of the Rheims Way in 1963, as detailed in chapter six.

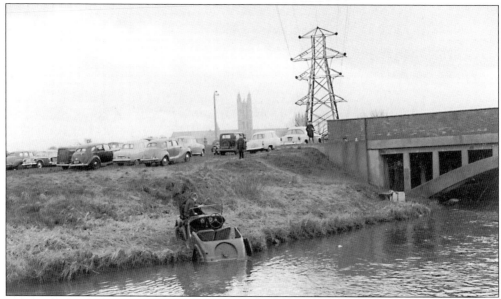

Children play on an abandoned and partially submerged sports car, just off Kingsmead Road, in February 1961. The road had been constructed in the late 1930s to link the suburbs of Northgate and St Stephen's and was part of an early attempt at giving Canterbury part of a proto-ring road. To the right is one of the 'new' bridges over the River Stour. These were built wide enough to carry a dual carriageway, but Kingsmead Road would never be dualled. To the left, cars are parked on waste ground, a common practice across the city at this time.

One of Canterbury's official car parks, on the former cattle market site off Upper Bridge Street, in May 1968. The photographer, Derek Stingemore, is peering through one of the replica gun loops in a facsimile city-wall defensive bastion, built in the late 1950s. The cattle market closed in 1955 and the site used for parking until the ring road – stage two – occupied the area (see chapter eleven).

Nine

New Construction in the 1960s

The modernist Longmarket development of 1961, as seen from St George's Street, in March 1967. Often ridiculed by being described as a series of shoeboxes, this overly minimalistic scheme was to few people's taste. The new building had replaced a complex of pre-fabricated shops and a few blitz-surviving buildings that occupied the site until the late 1950s, and which are shown in earlier chapters. The unloved complex was demolished in 1990 and replaced by an over-scale pastiche development, which polarized opinions even further.

The petrol forecourt and main showroom of Marlowe Motors in Rose Lane, c. 1961. The garage, built on the site of a smaller complex lost in the Blitz, had not long been officially opened by Jack Warner. An office block and further showrooms were built to the right of the existing development in 1965 and named Watling House. Both building phases were demolished in early 2001, as part of the Whitefriars development scheme.

New garage office and showroom buildings for Invicta Motors being constructed in Lower Bridge Street, during 1963. The site was already being used by Invicta as a collection of small garages and converted houses (see page 15). Now these were being demolished and the site redeveloped in stages, to minimize the disruption to the business. The new buildings were completed by October 1964. In the 1990s, Invicta consolidated their business on a site in Sturry Road (see page 97) and the Lower Bridge Street premises were converted into shops.

The nearly completed garage for P.D. Tobin Ltd, on the corner between Union Street and Union Place, in June 1961. The whole area, until recently covered with early nineteenth-century terraced housing, was divided into two designated areas on the Wilson development Plan. A strip parallel to Northgate, including this site, was earmarked for industrial development, whereas the rest of the area would be redeveloped for residential use. The north side of Union Street had been cleared in 1959 (see page 28), after which the street was widened, as can be seen in the foreground.

Bligh Bros Ltd, filling station and showroom in Dover Street, during the mid 1960s. The age of universal car ownership prompted the construction of small garages and filling stations all over the city and usually, terraced houses had to give way to them (see page 28). The Bligh Bros. premises were destined to be short lived. The building was pulled down in the mid-'70s, in advance of an office tower block development which was subsequently cancelled. The area is still undeveloped today.

The scaffolding-clad frame of the new Riceman's department store, rising up on the west side of St George's Lane, in 1961. Until the previous year, the site had been occupied by the buildings of the Simon Langton Boys' School (see page 69). A wall fragment from one of the demolished school buildings can be seen in the foreground. Riceman's was being constructed well back from the existing street frontage, to allow for later road widening. The new department store ignored the 'medieval scale' of the new 1950s buildings and heralded the arrival of the 1960s 'bigger is better' decade.

The new commercial vehicle showrooms, workshop and stores building for Caffyns Ltd, on the corner of Lower Chantry Lane and New Dover Road, during the month of its opening in September 1962. Caffyns already had older premises on the opposite corner of New Dover Road (off picture right), but wanted to expand to keep up with its main city competitors, namely Invicta Motors and Barretts. The building is now the Blockbusters video store.

Four-storey maisonette blocks on the south side of Union Street in March 1968. Designed by City Architect John Berbiers, they had been built on a site cleared of early nineteenth-century terraced houses in 1962 (see page 72). Further down the street and beyond the turning into Victoria Row, is the William IV public house, one of the few old buildings to have survived the demolition purge. Another pub on the same side of the street, the Union Castle, had not been so fortunate.

The brand new extension to the city council's old people's home, The Holt, just off Fisher Road in 1965. The original building, not seen here, was an eight-bedroomed house, probably built in the 1800s and set in $4\frac{1}{2}$ acres of land. Designed by City Architect John Berbiers, the new extension buildings won a top award in the local government good housing competition for 1965. The total cost of the new extension was £100,000. Both the old building and the 1960s extension, were demolished in 1988 and replaced by another senior citizens complex in a post-modernist design.

The modernist buildings of the University of Kent and Canterbury rise out of the mud during construction in February 1965. The complex is spread out on the high ground to the north of the city, off Giles Lane, and on an area once occupied by Brotherhood and Beverley Farms (see page 107). The picture, taken from the newly completed Physical Sciences Block, shows Eliot College taking shape. The first intake of undergraduate students was accepted in October of the same year.

The new £36,500 ambulance station on the east side of Military Road, just before its official opening by the Mayor, Councillor Ernest Kingsman in February 1965. Until the early 1960s, the Military Road frontage was crowded with early nineteenth century terraced houses (see page 72). The Canterbury Ambulance Service first started in 1945, with two ambulances that had been converted from vans by the Civil Defence in the war. By 1965, the service boasted seven modern ambulances and a total staff of twenty-five people.

Canterbury's new police station taking shape off the Riding Gate roundabout in February 1965. At this time, the £108,000 scheme was three months ahead of schedule and expected to open by the end of the year. The 'ultra-modern design' was faced in flint, to mirror the city wall opposite. The new building would house both the Canterbury Police Station and Divisional Headquarters, then residing in older buildings in Pound Lane and Kirby's Lane respectively.

The beginning of construction for the city's new fire station, on the east side of Upper Bridge Street, in November 1965. This was built to replace the existing station along Old Dover Road, housed in the former St Lawrence Farmhouse and a series of corrugated iron sheds, put on by the National Fire Service in 1943. The new complex was designed by Kent County Architect Mr E.T. Ashley-Smith and used some flint aggregate panels in its construction, similar to the new police station. The new fire station became operational in February 1967.

A new development of showrooms and offices, housed in a four-storey block on the east side of Upper Bridge Street, in June 1966. The recently completed fire station is just to the right. The new building, known as Lombard House, was built on a site once occupied by a range of single storey almshouses (see page 74). The picture, taken from the city wall, includes the trees of the former cattle market, now a car park. These would soon be lost for the construction of the ring road – stage two.

An overall view of the Christ Church College complex in the late 1960s, with the Cathedral and old city in the background. The vantage point used was the seven-storey student residential block. To the right is the modernist aluminium and glass roof of the college chapel. Christ Church College, an Anglican foundation for training teachers, was built within the precincts of the former St Augustine's Abbey and shared the site with the ruins of the once grand abbey church and its out-buildings.

The new Wolfson Library in flint and red brick, to the north of the main Cathedral building, in 1966. It had been built on top of the ruinous east arm of the former Infirmary Cloister, better known as the Dark Entry. It stands where the old monastic Chequer Building, or counting house, could once be found. This, however, had been pulled down in 1868. The only part of this building to have survived that act of Victorian vandalism, was its charming staircase turret, which can be seen beyond and above the new building.

The extensive commercial premises of Invicta Motors Ltd along Sturry Road. c. 1966. The complex had recently been extensively rebuilt and now included a tractor division, truck division, main parts department and filling station. At this time, their main cars division was at the Lower Bridge Street premises, in the city itself (see page 90). In the late 1980s, the entire Invicta operation was centred on the Sturry Road site, which was entirely rebuilt. This involved the demolition of some of the terraced houses seen here on the left.

Numbers 29 to 33 Watling Street, probably the finest and most successful marriage of old and new buildings in Canterbury. Occupying the sites of houses lost in the blitz, the in-fill developments either side of the early nineteenth-century house at No. 31, were constructed in 1964. The architect, Anthony Mauduit, has respected the scale of the existing buildings, whilst employing a modernist style for his in-fill structures. In 1966, this excellent scheme received a Civic Trust Award.

The buildings of the new Technical High School for Boys in Spring Lane, nearing completion in June 1967. At this time, the old boys tech was housed in the former Kent and Canterbury Hospital buildings in Longport (see pages 12 and 123). The need to build a new boys tech was identified in the Wilson Plan of 1951, but the site then earmarked for it was just off New Dover Road, where the Pilgrims Way School was later built instead. The boys tech is now known as the Geoffrey Chaucer School and has a mixed intake.

The impressive new headquarters for the Royal Insurance Group, on the east side of Lower Bridge Street, in April 1967. The building was opened by Lord Cornwallis, Lord Lieutenant of Kent and also chairman of the London board of the insurance group. Their old premises were at No. 29 High Street, on the corner into Stour Street. The cars in the foreground are parked on a demolition site once occupied by the old Co-operative store (see page 73). This site would soon be used for the ring road – stage two.

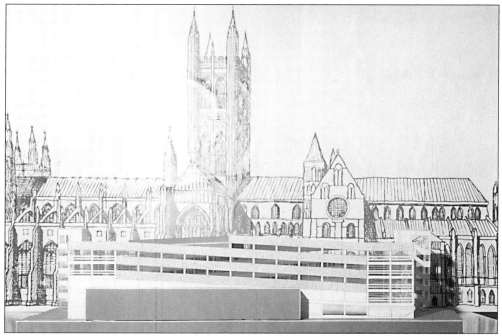

A model of the proposed multi-storey car park, with a backdrop depicting the cathedral, at an exhibition in March 1968. The multi-storey, completed in 1969 on a large site between Gravel Walk and Watling Street, has probably been the most controversial building in post-war Canterbury. Its stark 'brutalist' appearance and location within the city walls, has won it few supporters. Even those with little architectural knowledge feel that they are on safe ground by criticizing it. At the time of writing (July 2001), this unloved structure was only weeks away from demolition, as part of the Whitefriars scheme.

The skeleton of the new swimming pool on Kingsmead Road, taking shape in September 1969. Canterbury had been without a pool since the former outside swimming baths off Whitehall Road (Toddlers Cove) had been closed on health grounds in the early post-war years. Earlier plans to construct a swimming pool within the Dane John, were never realised. That scheme had glass walls to allow the bathers views of the city wall and mound. Even the Kingsmead plans were greatly scaled down from the original scheme, which included sunbathing terraces.

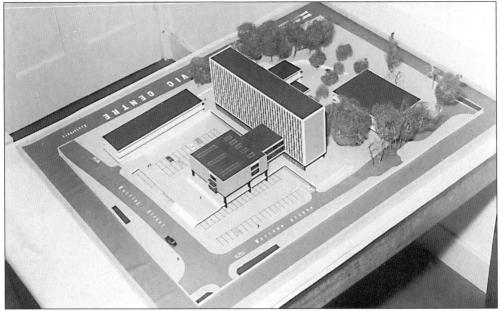

A detailed model of the Canterbury city centre development that never was. The model, being exhibited in October 1965, shows the proposed Civic Centre planned to be built on the Watling Street car park site, but also displacing the Regency buildings on the Dane John. Dreams for a Civic Centre on this site stretch back as far as the 1930s. Plans for the £800,000 scheme were halted by the government in May 1968, whose Royal Commission on Local Government would lose Canterbury its County borough status.

Ten
Scenes from the
1960s

A small cheerful CND protest group hand in a petition at the headquarters of the Canterbury City Council on the Dane John, during February 1960. The march, from the cathedral to the council offices, was led by the well-known 'Red Dean' Hewlett Johnson, seen second from the right. It is interesting to note that the good-natured protest reflects all age groups, but is dominated by senior citizens. At this time, these Regency buildings on the Dane John were under threat of demolition, to make way for a new Civic Scheme (see opposite page).

Canterbury city firemen tackle a blaze in the upper storeys of No. 78 Broad Street, in the spring of 1960. At the time, these were the premises of electronic components manufacturer, B.W. Cursons. The junction with Northgate can be seen beyond the firemen. Broad Street was on the route of the planned ring road, but would not have been widened until stage three of the construction. Buildings on the street's south east side were destined to be demolished, which would also have exposed the city wall. In any event, the ring road, stage three, never went ahead.

The annual city carol singing gathering in the Marlowe car park, at the St Margaret's Street end, in December 1961. This event was very popular in the early post-war years and usually attended by the archbishop, who gave the blessing. The archbishop was Michael Ramsey, newly installed that year. This gap in the building line was once occupied by the Royal Fountain Hotel, which had been destroyed in the June 1942 Blitz. Today, it is the site of the Marlowe Arcade Shopping Development.

One of Canterbury's infamous traffic bottlenecks, the St Dunstan's level crossing, in June 1962. Note the pro-railway advertisement, which if shown today, would surely attract some derisive graffiti! A class 71 electric locomotive is about to cross over St Dunstan's Street, probably with a coastal bound freight train (see page 82). The manually operated gates were replaced by automatic barriers in the early 1970s.

The west end of St Peter's Street, on a sunny summer's day in August 1962. The bunting is probably out for Cricket Week, the home of Kentish cricket being at the St Lawrence grounds on the other side of the city. Left, is part of the premises for Barretts of Canterbury Ltd. Built in 1938, this Art Deco style building was gutted in the last enemy raid on Canterbury, on 22 January 1944. Nevertheless, the frontage was repaired and the building remained until being replaced in the late 1970s.

A section of the city wall following its collapse into the former moat, August 1962. The location is just off the Riding Gate Roundabout, with the Victorian Riding Gate Bridge just visible beyond the debris. This part of the city wall had been badly damaged in the daylight raid of October 1944 and, as is evident, its early post-war repair was inadequate. The site was tidied up, but full restoration did not take place until 1970, when the Riding Gate itself and this section of wall were repaired using concrete sections faced with flint (see page 121).

A fragment of the medieval city wall, surviving at the junction of Burgate Lane and St George's Gate, on 14 January 1963. The abutting brick wall nearest the camera, is all that remains of a shop at number five St George's Gate, lost in the Blitz over twenty years earlier. Sadly, the medieval wall fragment would soon be demolished, as the site was needed for the St George's Street approach to the proposed St George's roundabout, destined to become part of the ring road construction, stage two (see page 117).

Activity in the West Station Coal Yard, during February 1963, despite the inclement weather. Domestic coal was regularly delivered here by rail, then distributed by a number of coal yard based merchants such as W.E. Pinnock Ltd and P.Hawksfield & Son. The snow-covered roofs of the Victorian and Edwardian houses in North Lane are clearly visible beyond the coal stays. The coal yard went out of use in the 1980s and today, the area is tightly packed with houses.

Children and teenagers eagerly wait for the carnival to pass-by, on the east side of Military Road, in July 1963. Behind is one of Canterbury's few post-war built pubs, the Leopards Head, opened in August 1959 to replace its blitzed predecessor. The short terrace of houses beyond is amongst the small number of older properties to have survived the demolition purge of the early 1960s (see page 72). By this time, many of the people seen here lived in newly built houses and maisonettes, built on the sites of the older slum-cleared dwellings

City council workmen and officers inspect the Riding Gate Bridge in February 1964, after a section of the superstructure had fallen onto the road beneath. Unfortunately, their inspection revealed cracks in the brick buttresses holding the bridge up. The cause was likely to be connected to the collapse of a large section of the city wall, immediately south of the Riding Gate, around eighteen months earlier (see page 104). The Riding Gate Bridge, new in 1883, was finally replaced in late 1970 (see page 121).

Drama on the St Peter's roundabout in February 1964. A loaded tanker lorry overturned as it negotiated the roundabout, spilling its flammable load. Quantities of sand have been applied in an effort to contain the spillage. Cables have also been attached to the chassis in readiness to right it. Sadly, this is still an all too frequent occurrence, usually caused by heavy lorries negotiating the roundabout too fast, having built up speed on the descent from London Road. Beyond is the now lost Holy Cross School.

Beverley Farm House, situated on the high ground to the north of Canterbury, in the early 1960s. The building was largely of medieval origin, with Victorian brick-built additions. In December 1963, the farmhouse and its surrounding land were taken over by the University of Kent and Canterbury, who would establish a modern campus on the former farmland in the mid-1960s (see page 94). In the meantime, the run down farmhouse was used as the university's academic and administrative centre. Its semi-derelict outbuildings, including an ancient barn, were all demolished.

A mid-1960s scene that has changed beyond all recognition today! This is the northern approach to the city, where Sturry Road meets Northgate at the traffic light controlled junction into Kingsmead Road (centre view). All of the elderly terraced houses crowding the street frontage, would all be demolished by the end of the decade (see page 78). Just visible in the background on the left, is the roof line of the Prince of Wales Youth Club. This was destroyed by fire in the 1970s. The garage, far left, was demolished in 1988 when the road junction became a roundabout, following the creation of Tourtel Road.

Simon Langton schoolboy Trevor Pinnock, at the piano in his Canterbury home in April 1965. This was around the time that he won an organ scholarship to the Royal College of Music. Later in 1973, Trevor went on to form a baroque ensemble known as The English Concert, performing and recording major works by eighteenth century composers such as Vivaldi and especially Handel. In June 1992, he was awarded the CBE, in recognition of his considerable musical achievements.

Canterbury's famous 1960s semi-professional group, the Wilde Flowers, at the rear of the ABC cinema in St George's Place, October 1965. At the time, the group were performing songs in between children's films at the Saturday morning cinema club. The line-up is, left to right; Robert Wyatt, Hugh Hopper, Brian Hopper and Richard Coughlan. Note the unnamed fan, complete with wig and psychedelic guitar case. Robert and Hugh would go on to play in Soft Machine, whereas Richard would become a founder member of Caravan.

The original line-up of Canterbury group Caravan, by the monument atop the Dane John Mound, in September 1968. They are, left to right, back row; Richard Sinclair, Pye Hastings, front row; David Sinclair, Richard Coughlan. During the following month, Caravan would record their debut album in London. The music of Caravan became part of what is known world-wide as the 'Canterbury Sound', usually characterized by odd time signatures, chord changes and a overall jazz influence.

The unmistakable faces of rock group Pink Floyd, prior to a gig at the old Marlowe Theatre in St Margaret's Street, during March 1969. The group were still licking their wounds following the departure of the main writer, visionary and LSD casualty, Syd Barrett. Of course, Pink Floyd would recover, and following their best selling album ' *Darker Side Of The Moon*' would go on to become one of the major stadium rock bands that would never again consider playing in Canterbury.

Cars ease their way through the flood water pouring out of Thannington Pumping Station following a burst water main, in February 1967. The location is the top end of Wincheap, where the suburb becomes what was once the village of Thannington. The four-storey block of flats and the road that serves it, Woodville Close, were constructed in the late 1950s, following the demolition of a large Regency period house (see page 22).

Surface car parking at Whitefriars, as seen from the vantage point of the newly constructed multi-storey car park, in December 1969. In the foreground is the wide expanse of Gravel Walk, built as the first stage of the aborted relief road, once destined to cross the city in parallel to the existing main street. The vast surface car park, once the site of the Simon Langton Boys School (see page 69), would see the construction of the Whitefriars Shopping Centre in the early 1970s.

Eleven

The Ring Road
Stage Two

Wincheap Green, looking in an easterly direction towards the Worthgate Place junction (left) and the houses of Pin Hill, in May 1968. Immediately behind the cameraman is the Wincheap Green roundabout and the limit of the first stage of the construction for Canterbury's ring road, completed in 1963. Now, stage two was about to be implemented. The partially white rendered corner building is the former Man of Kent public house, closed and awaiting demolition for the ring road. In the event, only the slate roofed Victorian extension was pulled down, with the seventeenth century portion (left) reverting to use as a house.

The late Victorian or Edwardian period houses at numbers 1 to 4 Pin Hill, in 1969, just prior to their demolition for the ring road. This would see Pin Hill become a dual carriageway. Note the temporary structure around the bay window of the nearest property. This was put in place following an impact from a car in November 1966. At the end of the terrace is the Man of Kent pub, seen in the opposite direction in the previous image. Far right is the start of the moat walk, then part of the Dane John.

The south-west side of Pin Hill, as it appeared prior to 1969. The detached house nearest, at No. 5, was the home of Frederick Richards, until its demolition for the ring road in 1969. Beyond are the rears of the substantial late Victorian town houses fronting Station Road East. Their rear walls and out-buildings would be lost to the ring road construction (see page 122). Just visible at the far end is the large depository warehouse of Pickfords Removal & Storage. It is the only building remaining from this scene today.

This delightful view is the moat walk between Pin Hill, Rhodaus Town and the city wall. It was part of the Dane John Gardens, the bulk of which is on the other side of the city wall ramparts. Construction of the ring road would mean the widening of both Pin Hill and Rhodaus Town to become dual carriageways. More significantly, it would mean the destruction of the moat and a considerable lobby being built up, in an effort to save this charming green area.

The beginning of the destruction of the moat in September 1968, as seen from the top of the city wall. Pin Hill on the right becomes Rhodaus Town as it curves around to the left. Even the protestors against the loss of the moat realised that Canterbury would choke with traffic unless the ring road was extended. Inevitably, the pro-car lobby won the day, as they always did in the 1960s. In the winter of 1968, the old moat exacted its last revenge by flooding and holding up work for some weeks.

Rhodaus Town – the moat and city wall ramparts, as seen from the Dane John Mound, c. 1967. This was the location of the city's Coronation celebrations back in 1953 (see page 35). On the far side are the premises of Rootes Ltd, automobile engineers and filling station (see page 33). The decision to lose the moat rather than the garage complex for the dualling of Rhodaus Town, was made for purely commercial reasons. The city owned the moat and besides, planners wanted to expose the city wall as an historical back drop to its ring road, in the same manner as seen in York.

Upper Bridge Street looking back towards Riding Gate roundabout, with Rhodaus Town beyond, c. 1967. Left is the concourse of the recently completed fire station (see page 95). Right, is the cattle market car park, soon to be lost when Upper Bridge Street was widened for the ring road. The Riding Gate Bridge and collapsed section of city wall, are just visible to the right of the roundabout.

The other end of Upper Bridge Street, as it approaches the traffic light controlled St George's crossroads, in 1968. At the crossroads, St George's Gate comes in from the left, St George's Place from the right and with Lower Bridge Street straight on. At the far end is the recently completed Royal Insurance Building (see page 99). Everything between it and the cameraman was destined to be demolished for the St George's roundabout, which would replace the crossroads in 1969.

The derelict frontage of No. 2 Upper Bridge Street, a once elegant town house, as it was in February 1966. It is the black-looking building, to the right of the Morris Minor Traveller, in the picture at the top of the page. Blighted by the ring road plans, the property had been abandoned and boarded up since the 1940s. Prior to the Second World War, it had been the offices of auctioneers Cooper & Wacher. In March 1966, a mysterious fire would break out in the roof of this long derelict building. It was finally pulled down, together with its neighbours, for the roundabout in 1969.

Buildings on the corner of Lower Bridge Street and St George's Place, at the St George's crossroads, in 1968. The group is dominated by the department store of G.Twyman & Son Ltd, who specialised in carpets, soft furnishings and men's clothing. To the left, is the shop of the Modern Floral Services Ltd at No. 14a Lower Bridge Street. The blitz damaged shop that had once occupied the gap between the florists and Twyman's, had been demolished in the early 1950s (see page 11).

A view from September 1968, of the corner between St George's Gate and Lower Bridge Street, showing buildings that could be found opposite those in the top picture. The tobacconist and stationers premises of Pettit & Son at No. 1 St George's Gate, was the only shop in that short thoroughfare to escape the Blitz unscathed. To the left is the single storey wooden shop of E.R. Bates & Son, gunsmiths, built into the blitzed ruins of their former shop at number three St George's Gate. The car park to the right was once the site of the Co-operative stores, demolished in 1961 (see page 73).

An overall view of St George's crossroads, taken from the new Royal Insurance Building, in 1968. Left is the Modern Florists, followed by Twyman's, with Pettit's and the former Co-op site opposite and to the right. Beyond the crossroads is Upper Bridge Street, with the cattle market car park on the right. Furthest left is the Lombard House office development (see page 96). Right are the modern shops in St George's Lane that would become victims of the Whitefriars redevelopment scheme of the late 1990s.

By October 1969, all of the buildings around St George's Crossroads had been demolished and the traffic re-directed onto a rudimentary roundabout, albeit with a temporary road surface. The picture was taken from the roof of the ABC Cinema in St George's Place. Twyman's once stood on the corner plot at the bottom right and Pettit's on the site beyond the crane in the middle. Both Upper and Lower Bridge Streets were now functioning as dual carriageways and the short St George's Gate thoroughfare now ceased to exist.

A terrace of late Georgian shops on the north west side of Lower Bridge Street, in October 1964. They had been built on a filled-in former moat area, in front of the city wall. Blitz damage from 1942 is clearly evident here. The premises of Tice & Co, heating engineers at No. 6 (far left) is a hastily erected post-war structure on the site of its blitzed predecessor. Dumbrells greengrocer (No. 5) is the surviving ground-floor portion of a once three-storey building. Next is the intact Dyson's sweet shop (No. 4).

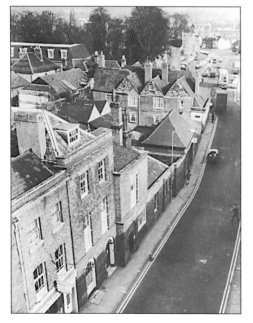

The buildings on the north west side of Lower Bridge Street are picked up again in this 1968 view from the Royal Insurance office block. The narrowness of the street compared to the appropriately named Broad Street further along, is graphically illustrated. Nearest the camera is the Hop Kweng Chinese restaurant (No. 2), followed by a doctors' surgery at No. 1 Lower Bridge Street. The three tiled gables just above centre view, are part of the rear elevation of the Saracen's Head public house, at the eastern end of Burgate.

The front of the Saracen's Head pub on the corner of Lower Bridge Street and Burgate, in 1968. It was built in the late seventeenth century and at the time of its construction, immediately abutted the south west tower of the Burgate City Gate. The site of the lost gate was now occupied by the white painted Burgate Motors premises, seen to the right. The wide expanse of Broad Street is in the foreground and clearly shows how the pub and other old buildings in Lower Bridge Street would have to give way for road widening.

The last pint being pulled inside the Saracen's Head, in February 1969, although everyone seems reasonably cheerful in spite of the sad occasion. The announcement of the pub's demise did not come suddenly. As long ago as June 1955, the local MP John Baker White had expressed his personal hope that the Saracen's Head could somehow be saved when the ring road was built. An eleventh hour suggestion by architect Anthony Swaine that half the pub be saved and thus still allow the road to be widened, fell on deaf ears.

The stripped premises of Burgate Motors Ltd, at No. 71 Burgate, awaiting it's imminent demolition in late 1969. The site of the recently pulled down Saracens Head is to the left. This three storey early nineteenth-century building was built on the site of the southern tower of the Tudor brick built city gate, the Burgate. The possibility that the Burgate Motors building might have preserved fabric from the lost city gate, will forever remain speculation, following its demolition.

Lower Bridge Street on a snowy day in early 1970, following the demolition of all the buildings on the far side of the street, as well as the Saracen's Head and Burgate Motors building on the corner into Burgate. The new carriageway is already in use, whereas the old carriageway is temporarily closed and in use as a car park. Right, are the premises of Invicta Motors Ltd, completed in stages in the early 1960s (see page 90). Furthest right is the shop of Brickies the butcher, to be demolished in 1974 for an extension to the Invicta premises.

Twelve

The Early 1970s

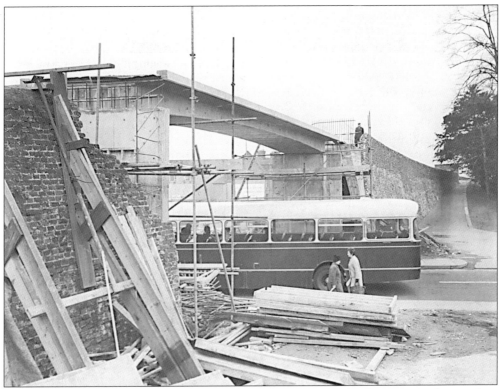

The concrete span and buttresses of the new Riding Gate Bridge being secured into place during February 1971. It replaced the previous wrought iron bridge that had been erected in 1883 and by the mid 1960s, was found to be unsafe (see page 106). The city wall immediately beyond the bridge, part of which had collapsed in the early 1960s, was also undergoing extensive repair. You can see the massive concrete frame of the new wall section directly below where the workman is standing on the bridge approach.

Professor Buchanan and his team try to cross the newly completed dual carriageway at Pin Hill, in January 1970. Author of the hugely influential 'Traffic in Towns' report, he had come to inspect the now complete second stage of the ring road construction. No sooner had he and his entourage left Canterbury East station, than they encountered the not inconsiderable problem of having to cross the new road. The large building to the right is the home of Cheyney & Co Ltd – scale makers.

The brand new concrete footbridge spanning Pin Hill, completed in 1971. Whether or not it was built as a direct result of professor Buchanan's experience is unclear. Nevertheless, the new bridge now safely carried pedestrians from the East station to the footpath on the city wall ramparts. One of the large late Victorian houses fronting the station approach had to be demolished to make the bridge's construction possible (see page 112).

The sad sight of the former St Andrew's Presbyterian church at Wincheap Green being demolished in March 1973. The church, which was something of a landmark for incoming rail passengers, had been carefully avoided during the construction of the Wincheap roundabout in 1963 (see page 65). It ceased to be a place of worship during the 1960s, after which it served various functions including that of a youth club. A developer purchased the redundant church and the Cheyney's premises behind (see opposite page). Despite their demolition, the proposed development never went ahead.

Demolition of another familiar and well loved Canterbury building – that of the former Kent and Canterbury Hospital complex at Longport, in 1972. Built in the grounds of St Augustine's Abbey, it later became the Technical College for Boys, following the construction of the new hospital at South Canterbury in 1937 (see page 12). The building became redundant once more when the new boys technical complex was built in Spring Lane during 1967 (see page 98). This later became the Geoffrey Chaucer School. Demolition of the former hospital, planned as early as the 1930s, could then finally be carried out.

One of the rarely photographed lost houses in Canterbury. This narrow mid Victorian property in Adelaide Place, is seen from the Castle Street junction in about 1971. It was being demolished, along with many other adjacent buildings, to free the site for development, including a suite of council offices. A former brewery complex in Stour Street, Cakebread Robey builders yard off Adelaide Place and several industrial buildings in Beer Cart Lane, all became victims of the same clearance. The site of this lost house remains empty today.

Late Georgian houses, at numbers 26 to 28 St George's Place, being prepared for demolition in July 1971. They were part of a short stretch of similar properties to have survived the Blitz. Even then, the frontage of No. 27 (centre building) had been blown away, which explains its modern appearance. Following clearance of the site, an office development called Rutland House was built here. Far left, are Caffyns Garage (demolished 1984) and Telephone House, now known as Becket House.

The dramatic new Midland Bank office and bank hall development in Gravel Walk, completed in 1972. It was built on a site once occupied by the Simon Langton Boys' School, but which for many years had been a massive surface car park (see page 110). Constructed in the same architectural style, the building to the left contains the main lobby and stairwells for the new Whitefriars shopping development. Its fascinating pyramid shaped skylights can just be seen above. All are due for demolition in 2002.

The large plot on the western corner of Watling Street and a widened Rose Lane, as seen from the multi-storey car park, in the early 1970s. The area is dominated by the overgrown rear garden of the Jacobean house fronting Watling Street (left), by this time, a solicitors office. Further along Watling Street is the white rendered rear elevation of a newly constructed office block. This is the site once occupied by two blitz damaged Jacobean houses (see page 19). The Brewer & Son greengrocer's shop, seen on page 73, once stood on the street corner site (bottom left).

The old premises of blind makers A.H. Amey & Son Ltd in Ivy Lane, at around the time of their closure in February 1975. Note the asbestos roof, added in the mid 1940s, following damage by incendiary bombs in the June 1942 Blitz (see page 11). The threat of compulsory purchase had hung over the business since about 1970. At this time, many small businesses were being 'encouraged' to re-locate to new industrial estates on the city outskirts. The City Council were also keen to expand the Longport coach park site, seen in the foreground. Demolition took place later the same year.

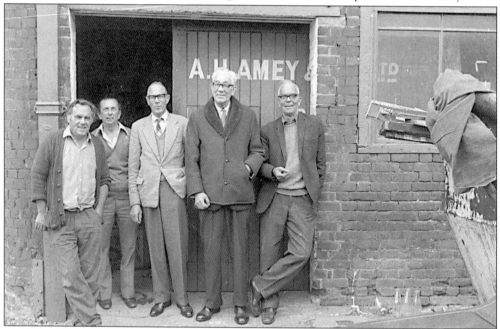

Employees of Amey's Blinds gather outside the old Ivy Lane premises at the start of the relocation procedure, in late 1974. They are, left to right; Johnnie Boylett, Ron Parker, Frank Fleet, Harry Crampton and Horace Meers. My grandfather Harry (real name Edward), joined the firm in 1924 as a delivery boy. This was the same year that Amey's bought the old oast in Ivy Lane. By the time of his retirement in 1974, he was a shareholder and board member. Grandad died in 1991.

Cheerful squatters about to be evicted by the police from Station Cottages, Station Road West, in March 1974. They had erected a banner that read; 'Homes for people, not for profit'. If you consider that these perfectly sound houses were otherwise empty and awaiting demolition, then they probably had a point! Station Cottages, a terrace of eight dwellings, had been built in the 1840s or '50s, as homes for railway workers at the adjacent station and coal yard (see page 105).

Numbers 53 and 54 Ivy Lane, completely derelict and threatened with demolition in November 1974. Literally hundreds of ordinary terraced houses had been pulled down in the 1960s. Some had been unsanitary, yet many more merely stood in the way of proposed road schemes. Very few people who were not directly affected, actually protested. However, by the mid 1970s, public attitudes had changed. Protest became more pro-active, as seen in the top image, and people were more aware of their heritage. Supported by the newly formed City Council Conservation Department, these houses were saved.

A row of old cottages at numbers 46 to 49 North Lane, either empty or boarded up, in October 1975. These houses had just been saved from demolition, following the cancellation of the third stage of the ring road. Much was changing. Local government re-organization in 1974 had robbed Canterbury of its autonomous county borough status. The new City Council immediately set up a conservation department, with the aim of preserving what remained of the city's secular heritage. The ring road's third stage, which would have required much demolition, was soon cancelled.

Typical '70s cars crowd the surface parking areas either side of Castle Street in November 1975. The vast area was once occupied by the gas works, which had been demolished in stages throughout the 1960s (see pages 70 and 79). In the '70s, the furthest site would see the construction of the Rosemary Lane multi-storey car park, which in accordance with the new thinking, would be low rise and screened from view by houses. The tannery buildings, dominating the background, are all threatened with demolition at the time of writing.